Management: Principles and Policy

Colin Carnall and Susan Maxwell

Management:

Principles and Policy

ICSA PUBLISHING · CAMBRIDGE

Published by ICSA Publishing Ltd
Fitzwilliam House, 32 Trumpington Street, Cambridge CB2 1QY, England

First published 1988
Second impression 1989

British Library Cataloguing in Publication Data
Carnall, C.A. (Colin A.)
   Management.
   1. Management
   I. Title   II. Maxwell, Susan M.
   658

ISBN 0-902197-58-4

Library of Congress Cataloging in Publication Data
Carnall, C.A. (Colin A.)
   Management: principles and policy/Colin A. Carnall and Susan M.
   Maxwell.
      p.   cm.
   Bibliography: p.
   Includes index.
   ISBN 0-902197-58-4
   1. Management.   I. Maxwell, Susan M.   II. Title.
   HD31.C349 1988
   658.4—dc19   87-36003
                                                            CIP

Designed by Geoff Green
Typeset by Tradespools Ltd., Frome, Somerset
Printed in Great Britain by St. Edmundsbury Press, Bury St. Edmunds, Suffolk

Contents

Preface

This book is designed mainly for those preparing for the
Management: Principles and Policy paper of the Institute of
Chartered Secretaries and Administrators. It reflects the practical
approach adopted by this Institute in its management curriculum.
Kurt Lewin once said 'There's nothing so practical as a good theory'.
Following this thought, we have selected ideas and concepts from
the vast literature on management with practical application in
mind.

The book should prove valuable to all professional students up to
university degree level and on many degree courses where
management forms a part of the curriculum. It has been designed to
give an up-to-date introduction to the main themes of management,
with case-study illustrations to enhance the practical aspects of the
book.

The authors wish to thank many of the course members at Henley
– The Management College, for their comments and contribution to
some of the ideas presented herein.

The authors are indebted to June Sebley who word-processed the
often illegible manuscript, paying attention both to content and
much of the detail. Needless to say all errors are the responsibility of
the authors.

Colin Carnall
Susan Maxwell

Chapter 1

Management work and managerial performance

Introduction

In today's world, managers face complex and changing pressures and opportunities. They must ensure the efficient use of resources and, at the same time, the long-term effectiveness of the organisation for which they work. Effectiveness in a changing environment includes being able to identify the right things to do in the future (the right products and services to offer, the appropriate technologies to exploit, the best procedures and structures to introduce, and the most appropriately qualified people to employ) and ensuring the flexibility and adaptability necessary for change to be achieved.

Implementing change effectively has been, and seems likely to remain, one of the main challenges facing managers, in both the private and public sector, in manufacturing, banking, health care and education, often in very stark circumstances. Sales and profitability may be falling rapidly. A merger bid may lead managers to review performance and plans as part of an attempt to fight it off. Deregulation causes dramatic changes in many sectors. Central government expenditure pressures can create serious constraints in the public sector, often with dramatic effects on budgets. Privatisation and competitive tendering have led many organisations to develop greater commercial awareness and discipline in their staff. Managers are concerned about value for money, the development and marketing of new products and services, and flexibility, whether of design, manufacture or service delivery, or in organisational structure and management style. Managers are increasingly concerned about product or service performance and quality. Customers and clients are ever more vocal and critical. This applies across the whole spectrum of organisation. Motor-car manufacturers use quality and reliability as a selling feature of cars. In education 'parent involvement' and 'parent power' have become important considerations.

The main focus of management is switching from internal concerns to a balanced focus on both internal and external matters. This book is concerned with the management of enterprises internally (organisation structures, managerial effectiveness, motivation, coping with change) and externally (planning and implementing new strategies, managing corporate affairs and image). We now turn to two illustrative case studies before examining these issues in the light of current management ideas and thinking.

Case study: ABF Ltd

ABF Ltd manufactures a range of plastic products and employs a total of 350 people. The present managing director has worked with the company for 21 years, ten as managing director. All his senior colleagues are long-service employees. In 1986 a team of consultants reviewed company procedures, particularly in manufacturing. There had been growing concern over indirect labour costs. The consultants were asked to look at the following areas:
1. Planned maintenance.
2. Quality levels and quality assurance.
3. Utilisation of machine setters and technicians.
4. Information systems.
5. Manufacturing organisation.
As this work proceeded a number of very significant changes were being introduced. However, the commitment of top management to change was low. In particular the managing director was content to let the consultants lead the way.

The company was also experiencing a range of what we often refer to as 'human relations problems'. Confrontation between managers was a regular occurrence. Often managers would adopt an aggressive approach in discussion, taking an entrenched position. Conflict between the production director and staff in the sales department was particularly prevalent.

Communication was very poor. Rarely were the production departments notified of priority orders. Often they would hear of a new machine purchase or a new product launch only days beforehand. Managers tended to treat subordinates autocratically, issuing orders but allowing no discussion. Ideas tended to be suppressed, particularly from younger employees. People were expected to conform to 'the way we have always done things around here'. Managers appeared to feel that change was both a threat and an implied criticism of their own personal performance.

Managers seemed obsessed with objectives set years ago. For example, in production, the main concern was with the sales value of output and with efficiencies. No concern was directed at the quality of output nor at producing to schedule. Thus deliveries were often late and there was a high level of returned goods. Attempts to start discussion of these latter problems led to intensely defensive reactions by production management.

The company went through a period of strong growth after 1976 but profits stagnated over 1982–86. Delegation to middle and junior management was poor. No management training ever took place. Promotion was entirely from within. The managing director expressed the view that anyone promoted 'will know what to do or else we should not have promoted them'. Discouraged to take the initiative or to bring forward ideas and lacking in confidence, many junior or middle managers tended to leave decisions to directors. In consequence, the directors felt that they were unable to take effective decisions and were often vocal in their criticism of these managers.

The managing director tended not to listen to other people's views. Thus there was very little exchange of ideas. People did not go to him to discuss problems, frustrations and so on. It seemed that both he and they felt that discussing attitudes and feelings was difficult and therefore avoided it as a means of protecting the other person's sensitivities. Thus there was very little testing of views. Appraisals of senior staff were not carried out. Indeed recording performance reviews on paper was seen to be counter-productive. However, the managing director had, and was known to have, strong views about individuals and often discussed them at length with other senior colleagues. It seems he liked confirmation of the views he felt unable to confirm with the individual. This meant that he formed views of people he did not share with them. In conversations with those individuals he gave the impression that he did not trust them. The individuals felt they could not approach him to discuss this because he would avoid that type of discussion.

For the changes in information systems, manufacturing organisation and maintenance systems the consultants have proposed to be sustained there is a clear need to develop a more positive attitude to change. Yet the 'vicious circle' the behaviour of senior management has created makes that all the harder to achieve. Managerial and organisational effectiveness are clearly essential: managerial effectiveness to provide the leadership and motivation needed; organisational effectiveness to provide for the necessary resources and adaptability to face future change.

Case study: The administrators

Argyris (1982) provided an excellent example which is considered here. A group of senior university administrators attending an executive course considered a case study of a particular college which included a set of recommendations for the future of the college, produced by a working group of senior academics and administrators from the college. The working group had been asked for 'concrete recommendations' by the principal of the college. The course members were asked to evaluate the recommendations produced by the working group. Criticising the recommendations, course members expressed the view that the recommendations were vague, cliché-ridden, the typical output of a committee that had not been well briefed.

Such an evaluation of working groups, working parties or committees is not uncommon, and seems to be based upon several assumptions about organisations and about people. The first is that giving people specific goals will lead them to actions which are more relevant to the task (in this case, to produce more specific recommendations). The second is that clear goals will motivate people, or if not, will at least make it easier to confront them on the quality of their performance. Third, it is assumed that in order to control performance effectively it must be monitored objectively. Underlying these assumptions is the fear that people will not obey, follow the rules, perform their tasks. Many managers see rules, regulations, systematic procedures, objective performance monitoring and control as the basis for certainty. So far so good! But implicit in this is the belief that rules, systems, monitoring and control cannot themselves bring about consequences that are counter-productive, that obstruct progress, that make it hard to 'get things done'. Yet we all know this to be false. When we think of bureaucracy we tend also to think of the 'red tape' meaning of that word.

Here we refer to what Merton (1940) has called the 'dysfunctional' consequences of bureaucracy and what March and Simon (1958) refer to as its 'unintended consequences'. For Merton (1940) a bureaucratic structure exerts constant demands upon officials to be methodical and disciplined. To operate successfully there must be reliability, conformity and discipline. However, adherence to the rules, originally conceived as a means, becomes transformed into an end in itself:

Discipline, readily interpreted as conformance with regulations, whatever the situation, is seen not as a measure designed for specific purposes, but becomes an immediate value in the life-organisation of the bureaucrat.

This emphasis, resulting from the displacement of the original goals, develops into rigidities and an inability to adjust readily. Formalism, even ritualism, ensue with an unchallenged insistence upon punctillious adherence to formalised procedures.

This may be taken to the extent that conformity to the rules obstructs the purposes of the organisation, known to us, familiarly, as 'red tape'.

To return to our example, how can we explain the apparent paradox? Remember that the original diagnosis was that the working party recommendations were vague and unusable, and that more specific goals and directions, combined with methods of monitoring and controlling performance, would overcome this difficulty. However, should such a strategy be implemented, the members of the working party may feel mistrusted and constrained. In any event, faculty members and administrators within a college are likely to pursue different ends and not work together well on critical issues. There is a need for integration between two disciplines, the members of which are trained in different ways, work to different rules, with different methods and styles, and who are likely to emphasise different views of the college. There might well be advantages in keeping goals vague. Specific goals might be interpreted as limiting and not allowing the freedom to think creatively. Specific goals may result in emotional reactions which inhibit performance. Thus actions which appear rational (setting specific goals) may lead people to produce what might be called counter-rational consequences.

These counter-rational consequences can emerge in three ways. First, individuals may distance themselves from the tasks in hand and the responsibilities involved. Not feeling any personal responsibility for producing the problem, they do not see it as their responsibility to solve it. Second, tacit acceptance may develop that the 'counter-rational' behaviour is 'undiscussable'. Where behaviour appears to be disloyal, there seems to be a tendency to see it as difficult to talk about openly – so difficult that all agree that the issue is 'taboo', in principle undiscussable. Finally, people may prefer counter-productive advice, that is to say, advice which reinforces the counter-rational behaviour. Thus, on the course we have been discussing, members suggested that the college president should play a game of deception in order to save face for himself and the faculty, and in order to keep his options open. They proposed that he accept the report, thank the working party, and at the same time arrange for a new committee, or implement specific action. Such behaviour would, of course, reinforce the undiscussability of the problem, and the distancing of the working party members from the issue at stake. It is clearly a form of collusion aimed at avoiding making the issues, or the working party's difficulties, explicit.

It is important for us to recognise that, by counter-rational, we do not mean irrational or emotional, although counter-rational behaviour may be emotional. Counter-rational behaviour may be highly rational from the point of view of the individuals concerned, given their situation.

Sources of ineffectiveness

People in organisations, whether representing themselves, or their groups, tend to advocate views and positions with a degree of certainty which discourages further enquiry. Moreover, they tend to act in ways which inhibit the expression of negative feelings. We often talk of the need to 'sweeten the pill' or not to overdo criticism in case people are 'upset' by it. Sometimes we offer presentations in such a way as to emphasise that there is nothing new or radical in a set of proposals. People appear to design their behaviour to appear 'rational'. Thus they focus upon what they argue to be necessary and attainable goals, realistic means and clear objectives – all in order to suppress the issue that might upset others. Moreover, people tend to control meetings to maximise winning, minimise losing, minimise the expression of negative feelings and to keep others rational.

People attempt to 'distance' themselves, to treat the issues and events as 'undiscussable' and to offer advice which, whilst ostensibly aimed at increasing rationality actually inhibits rationality. All of this tends to hinder the production of valid information for diagnosis and decision-making. Yet these behaviours are most prevalent just when valid information is needed – when people are dealing with difficult and threatening problems. We are dealing with a powerful set of individual, group, organisational and cultural forces which are mutually reinforcing. These forces create contradictions. Yet success can, and does, occur. But this will be based on routine performance, on stability. All of this can mean that people do not feel it necessary to pay attention to the deeper issues until the impact of these contradictions is so powerful that the stability is itself under threat. Now the organisation is seen to be in crisis. Drastic action is possible, 'turnaround' becomes the objective. Just such a situation may be developing at ABF Ltd. There the tendency not to discuss performance directly and openly is powerfully sustained by the behaviour of the managing director. Ironically enough, behaviour aimed at protecting peoples' sensitivities does exactly the opposite and leads to distrust.

This book will be concerned with the sources of ineffectiveness in organisations. By attempting to analyse and understand them it is intended to lay the basis for improving the ways in which they can be managed. Change is a key concern of the modern manager. It will be seen that ineffectiveness is both the 'enemy' of and the target of efforts to achieve change. It is the 'enemy' of efforts to achieve change in that ineffectiveness makes it harder to generate commitment to change or even an understanding of the need for change in the first place. Ineffectiveness is, or should be, a target of change in that if change can be used as a means of improving effectiveness then the future management of change can be made so much easier. For example, if a new computer is being installed to reduce the costs of processing a range of data then 'success' might be seen as cost reduction alone. Much better would be the wider view that the management of change develops a better understanding of the organisation and its problems amongst staff *and* is used as an opportunity to improve the work situation for them. Thus new computers can be used as a chance to review procedures, job content and work conditions. Job enrichment (see Chapter 3 below) might be possible. If organisation changes are managed effectively, the groundwork can be established for longer-run effectiveness and adaptability. Later on in this book practical ways will be examined of managing the situations described in the two case studies in this chapter so as to achieve effectiveness through organisational change.

Leadership and 'excellence'

Another way of thinking about how to encourage organisational change is to consider the management cultures many now argue to be emerging in 'excellent' companies. A number of books reviewing the characteristics of excellent companies have been published, notably *In Search of Excellence* by Peters and Waterman (1982), and more recently *A Passion for Excellence* by Peters and Austin (1985). Other books include Rosabeth Kanter's *The Change Masters* (1983). These books suggest that effectiveness is more likely to emerge from organisational cultures which encourage the following:
1. Accountability. This word is being used more and more when discussing management problems and practices. Where once we meant the fiduciary accountability of the board of directors to the

shareholders, we now refer to something quite different. We now refer to direct and personal accountability for performance. The stress is upon the individual manager and the performance of his* unit or team. Clearer accountability and tighter central control of finance and strategy have gone hand in hand with decentralisation of activities and resources to unit level. If the 1960s and 1970s was the era of 'involvement' in management books, the 1980s is the era of the individual. If we are now seeing the 'failure of collectivism' as both moral philosophy and organising principle we are also experiencing the re-emergence of individualism.

2. Synergy. This is the capacity to get co-operation and collaboration. People increasingly question instructions. Professionals expect to have a say in what they do. In consequence, effectiveness cannot be ensured by 'fiat'. Coercion may well generate compliance, but will fail to produce effort or creativity. Thus it is that the task of management includes the skills of achieving co-operation and collaboration. Moreover, much work demands the efforts of people drawn from varying technical disciplines, such as engineering, chemistry, metallurgy, marketing, accounting, and so on. Managing the process of getting things done often demands co-operation.

3. Cross-cultural skills. In all organisations we work with people from a diversity of backgrounds. Whether we are looking at a large public service organisation in an urban environment or the various facilities of a multinational corporation, we deal with cultural diversity. Management development involves developing what managers do. Thus, building the cross-cultural skills for handling this diversity is important. We shall see that these skills emerge from developing the skill of empathy, but more of that later.

4. Managing interfaces. Management involves the skills of co-ordinating the deployment of people, information, resources and technology in order that work can be carried out effectively. Managers in manufacturing, the public services, in charities and schools are all exhorted to this end in books, journals, newspaper articles and television programmes. Yet managers spend most of their time engaged in fragmented, and often problem-solving activities (see Stewart 1982; Mintzberg 1973). The nature of management work seems to comprise the resolution of problems arising from lack of co-ordination rather than the planned and

*Throughout this book the masculine form is used purely as a stylistic convenience. 'He' in all cases means 'he or she'

systematic pursuit of co-ordination. Our knowledge of the circumstances of work is fragmented and incomplete. And thus interface problems are common. Thus people concerned to carry out a task can find that the necessary resources, information or equipment are not available.
5. Financial realism. When one of the present authors worked as an engineering designer he often made design choices on technical but not commercial or economic grounds. The cost implications of decisions were not considered during the design process. In an increasingly competitive world this approach has become recognised as outmoded. Finance is a crucial input to any organisation – not the only one, or even the most important, but one which must be confronted in decision-making. Effective or 'excellent' organisations appear to be characterised by managers taking financial issues properly into account alongside other issues such as technical or marketing factors.

If these are some of the characteristics of effective or 'excellent' organisations, how can managers encourage them? To understand this it is necessary to understand how managers work. In the next section we turn to an examination of managerial performance and managerial work.

Managerial performance

Managerial performance is a combination of knowledge and skill applied in practice. Management is about 'getting things done', about action. Managerial work is surrounded by circumstances which create problems including uncertainty, incomplete information, change in the environment or elsewhere in the organisation, and conflict. Mintzberg (1973) has developed a comprehensive empirical picture of the nature of managerial work through observing and recording what managers actually do. He describes the managerial job in terms of roles (see Fig. 1.1). From his empirical

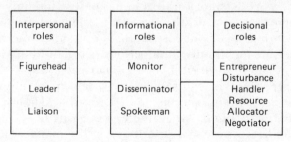

Fig. 1.1 Managerial roles.

work Mintzberg characterises managerial jobs as follows:
1. They are remarkably similar and can be described in ten roles (see Fig. 1.1) and six sets of working characteristics.
2. Much managerial work is challenging and non-routine, but every manager has some routine and regular ordinary duties.
3. A manager is both a generalist and a specialist.
4. Information is an important part of his power.
5. The major pitfall for the manager is having to be superficial because the workload is too high.
6. Management science has little effect on how the manager works because when under work pressure he fragments activity and uses verbal communication, making it difficult for management scientists to help.
7. The management scientist can only break this 'vicious circle' with real understanding of the manager's job, and access to the manager's own views of the help he needs.

The six characteristics relate to the following:
1. The quantity and pace of the manager's work.
2. The patterns of the activities.
3. The relationship in work between action and reflection.
4. The use of different communications media.
5. The relationships with contacts.
6. The interaction between rights and duties.

Mintzberg (1973), Stewart (1967), Dubin and Spray (1964), and Horne and Lupton (1965) all confirm from empirical studies that managers' workloads are substantial. Managers work at an unrelenting pace. This is because the job is inherently open-ended and the manager never finishes his work.

Managerial work is characterised by brevity, variety and fragmentation. The manager is never able to concentrate on one aspect of his job alone or for any length of time. The trivial and the important are mixed so that mood and tone shift and change continually. Mintzberg found that half of the activities of five chief executive officers (CEOs) took nine minutes or less and only 10 per cent lasted more than an hour. The manager is seldom able or willing to spend much time on any one issue. He is constantly interrupted. Rosemary Stewart found only nine periods of a half-hour without interruption in a four-week study of 160 managers!

The manager seems to stress the active element of his work–activities that are current, specific, well defined and non-routine attract more of his attention. For example, processing most mail and reading written reports are low-priority jobs. The manager may be seen as the conductor of the orchestra and conversely as a puppet pulled by hundreds of strings. To find out the extent to which managers controlled themselves, Mintzberg analysed whether in each activity managers were active or passive, and found only a small proportion of active work and that managers spent much time reacting. However, the initial construction of the manager's job may have included decisions to allow these reactions and passive participations as a way of keeping up a flow of work and ensuring the involvement of others in the management process.

Let us turn now to the ten managerial roles.

The interpersonal roles

Figurehead

In this role the manager operates as the representative of the organisation both externally and internally. For example, the chairman will accept an award for industry or safety, the marketing manager takes customers to a sporting event, or the head of a department attends an employee's wedding. Mintzberg found that about 12 per cent of a manager's time was spent on these seemingly trivial but actually important contributions to the smooth functioning of the organisation.

Leader

This role is a function of the responsibility the manager has for the people and their work. This responsibility may be direct, such as in recruiting and dismissing, or indirect, such as in motivating and encouraging people.

Liaison

Both Stewart and Mintzberg found that managers spend 50 per cent of their time with peers and people outside their units. The range of contacts includes subordinates, clients, business associates, superiors (if any), suppliers, managers of other units or organisations, government and trade-association officials and unconnected individuals. Managers use these contacts to build up an internal database of information and to build connections beyond the boundaries of their operations.

Informational roles

Knowledge is power. The contacts of the manager carry data to him and away to other contacts. As a hub or centre of such a data-gathering network, the manager can be better informed than any of his informants because he processes the data into information which assists good 'hunches', informed guesses, and intuition.

These roles relate both to the receiving and transmitting of information. The manager is a 'nerve centre' of the organisation as he has access to internal information and is an access point to external information.

Monitor

Internally he taps pressures, ideas and trends, reports and observations. Here Mintzberg means scanning the environment for gossip, incident, hearsay and speculation and integrating this as information. This enables the manager to understand what is taking place in the organisation and its environment. The information is needed to detect changes, identify problems and opportunities and build up general knowledge so as to be an informed disseminator and decision-maker.

Disseminator

In this role the manager shares and distributes the collected information to those without access who are within the unit or organisation. The disseminator also relays information, both factual and 'value', between subordinates. Factual information can be tested as to its validity and includes ideas, trade gossip and instant communication. Information about 'values' deals with preferences and beliefs of what 'ought' to be. Values are not right or wrong; the disseminator transmits them into the organisation to guide subordinates in making decisions.

Spokesman

In this role the manager acts as the channel of communication to outsiders, perhaps in a speech as part of a lobby or pressure group in providing specifications to a supplier or credit terms to a purchaser. Many of these cross-boundary activities are with the 'stakeholders' (see Chapter 10) in the organisation and are concerned with social responsibility. The manager operates as an expert in the field of the organisation's activity.

Decisional roles

Information is seen as the input to decision-making and the manager plays a major role in decision-making systems. Mintzberg describes this as the power to commit resources. The senior manager is the nerve centre with the only full and complete picture vital to strategically sound decisions.

Entrepreneur

Writers such as Pollard (1965) and Bendix (1956) have made distinctions between managers and entrepreneurs. Entrepreneurs take risks, handle uncertainties, make the initial decision over objectives and the firm's direction, and innovate. They seem to reoccur when the climate is dynamic and changeful as they harness new technologies to productivity by revolutionising methods and processes. Mintzberg's entrepreneurs adapt their units to changing conditions in the environment by taking up new ideas and creating climates and structures that encourage development of innovations. This process is usually a series of small decisions that allows slow assimilation rather than confrontations and abrupt changes. A chief executive will be sponsoring dozens of projects spread over every function and department of the organisation from technical processes to human resource management and public relations and, almost more important, he will integrate them.

Disturbance handler

This is the role that does not initiate change: it is the involuntary response and the attempt to minimise the uncertainty and solve the crises that arise in even well-managed organisations. When subordinates cannot agree amongst themselves, they approach the manager; when no one knows how to handle a problem, it passes along to the manager; when a crisis is perceived, the manager must take charge. Specialists do specialist work while the generalist manager handles general disturbances.

Resource allocator

The manager decides who shall get what in his organisational unit from his own time and attention to funding. This role also designs structures and divides and co-ordinates work. Decisions are made while the manager is aware of consequences and interrelations so

that power is not fragmented and tactics fulfil strategy. The decisions are very complex because:
1. They have impact on each other.
2. They must be acceptable to the participants.
3. Resources must not be over- or under-extended.
4. Costs and benefits have to be understood.
5. Delays in approval can be costly or destructive.
6. Quick judgement can be ill-considered.
7. Rejection is discouraging to workers.
8. The information available is never complete.

Negotiator

Negotiation takes up much managerial time and energy. Many are routine but all require careful consideration and skill. Mintzberg identifies two different aspects of this role which he believes is vital to management as it involves so many of the other roles: an 'equal footing, no advantage' setting; and a 'listen to the arguments but state own demands' setting. Negotiation is an important part of the manager's job.

The managerial job

The above identification and analysis of managerial roles cannot describe the whole but neither can a manager function unless he fulfils these roles in some degree. This is the real difficulty in team management which requires very careful reintegration and effective communication. Different managers spend different amounts of time on different roles.

To be effective a manager requires the following:
1. Self-knowledge and insight.
2. Understanding of the managerial job.
3. Timely and controlled responses to the pressures and dilemmas which apply.

The manager must also find ways of dealing with common bottle-necks which revolve round the overload/delegation/loss of control dilemma. The manager must find a systematic way of sharing information to enable subordinates to assist in decision-making.

He must code, quantify or analyse matters requiring attention to establish real priorities, see trends and patterns against the whole picture, and so devote time to real issues. This includes using specialists and advisers who have the time to investigate issues, make models and test propositions. The well-known planning dilemma is that managers have the authority and the information, and analysts the time and the technology. Neither managers nor analysts necessarily possess both! A manager must gain control of his own time by turning obligations to advantage and turning what he wants to do into what he is obliged to do. For example, making a speech is an opportunity to boost public relations, employee morale, pass on information and make wishes known non-specifically (i.e. generally, so that personal feelings do not get in the way).

Concluding comment

Many of the issues examined in this chapter will be considered again in later chapters. The most important point here is to emphasise that management is about creating and sustaining effectiveness. The managerial job is complex and demanding. Managers always have opportunities to improve things, whatever their level in the organisation. Of course the higher up the organisation, the greater the discretion to take the initiative to achieve change. But all managers have some discretion. This book will be concerned with understanding what managers can actually do to achieve improvement and change.

Chapter 2

Managerial accountability

Introduction

Managers are responsible for the work of other people. In effect a manager is authorised (either by a superior or through a formal job description) to delegate work to his staff. For a manager to be held accountable by a superior for the quality of the work done by a subordinate, two basic conditions have to be met; the manager must be able to decide what tasks will be delegated to the subordinate, and what resources will be allocated to the subordinate to carry out those tasks; and the manager cannot properly be accountable for the work of a subordinate who in the manager's judgement is below the level of competence necessary for getting the delegated work done.

In this context, the authority attached to a managerial position gives the right to exercise power within socially established limits. In many instances, the right extends to applying positive or negative sanctions (rewards or punishment) to subordinates, depending upon the quality of their behaviour. However, in practice, this does not work in a straightforward manner. Managers are expected to develop and train their staff and therefore, in practice, the second of the conditions listed in the previous paragraph is rather 'fluid'.

How managers are authorised to have power is an important question. In many countries legislation influences the way in which public and private sector enterprises are run, causing variations between countries and political systems. In a democracy of the kind found in Britain and North America, the power of the government is authorised by the group of electors on whose behalf the power is being used, thereby making that power legitimate. Indirectly, this also applies to companies in the private sector, governed by the constraints built into company law, employment law, and so on. These laws give certain powers to employers which permit the exercise of power over their managers and employees within limits. Similarly, the directors of a company are obliged to manage the company in the best interests of the shareholders. However, therein lies a number of issues regarding the efficacy of shareholder control (see Thomas 1973). Power, however, should not be seen purely as the right to apply sanctions to others. In practice, it is the quality of individuals or groups which enables them to influence the behaviour of other individuals (singly or collectively) in such a way that those with influence are helped to fulfil their own aims. It is the quality of a manager that gets others to act, to work, and to do things on his behalf. Thus the sources of power will include the professional and personal credibility of the manager concerned.

The operational core and its organisation

Every enterprise, public or private, needs to be clear about its 'operational core'. This is the part of the enterprise which directly produces outputs. It involves the development of goods or services, their production and their presentation to clients, or markets for sale or delivery. In manufacturing production, direct output is delegated to factory management. In design and research, output may be provided higher up in the organisation by way of presentations to senior management, with assistance from subordinates. In selling, a manager and a subordinate may share responsibility for direct output, each working with different levels of the customer's organisation.

These operational activities can be divided into specific tasks which can be assigned by managers to their subordinates to achieve, in terms of definable outputs. When the task is completed, the output can be observed. Such tasks are determined by the objectives of the enterprise and the operational activities which the senior management group has decided shall be carried out in pursuit of those objectives. The objectives of a business, set and controlled by its senior management group, will need to include the kind of goods and services to be provided, an outline of the clients or market to be served, and the general direction in which the goods and services should be designed and developed. Once these have been set, then the chief executive can organise the business to carry out operational activities in support of them, and will be held accountable for development, production and sales or delivery activities, and for co-ordinating them.

Since research, design and development tasks are concerned with modifying existing products or services, or developing new ones, it makes sense to organise these tasks into departments or sections based on projects or activities concerned with developing the same or related products or services. This implies that development should be concerned with finding means to satisfy the needs of consumers, and should not leave all its consumer contacts to the sales department. For example, valuable information can be obtained from test departments, quality departments and customer service departments.

Similarly, the production of goods and services may also be organised in product or service groupings to take advantage of specialisation, the benefit of which may otherwise be lost if the tasks are grouped according to customers or markets. However, the grouping of operational tasks in the sales and marketing (or service-providing) activities of the business by consumer groups or markets is thoroughly logical as a means of organisation. Moreover, many large organisations may also choose to organise by geographical area.

In analysing the activities involved in the direct output (actual production) of an end-product or service (or part of it), Elliott Jacques (1976) identified three different situations:

1. In manufacturing enterprises, with, say, mass production by hourly-paid operators, the operators produce the direct output, and the managers concern themselves solely with the delegation and control of direct-output tasks.
2. In most research work, in some selection work, or in district nursing, for example, the person working on the direct output may be assigned subordinates as assistants. This model of the person engaged on direct output being a manager at the same time is typical of the organisation of professional work.
3. In some sales situations, the sales manager delegates the direct-output activity of selling to a group of clients to a salesman, but once or twice each year visits the clients to deal with contacts at a higher level than the salesman can, in order to give him support. The sales manager may then settle with the managing director a range of sales policies, for example on prices, minimum order levels, service, and so on, within which the subordinate then carries on selling to the client's buyer.

Supporting activities and lateral relationships

So far we have been concerned primarily with manager–subordinate relationships and the two-way communications involved with them in the operational spine of the business. In addition, however, we must examine the organisation of activities provided in support of operational activities, these involving a wide range of lateral relationships with differing degrees of accountability and authority. Whilst accountability is related to outcomes, the authority needed to match it in a lateral relationship is concerned partly with the task, and partly with the sanctions which can be exercised by the occupant of one post towards the occupant of a laterally connected post in the organisation.

With regard to the initiation of tasks, the strongest degree of authority is that of being able to order another person to carry out a task, any failure to do so being evidence of negligence or misconduct. A lesser degree of authority is that of trying to persuade another to perform a task (with the other not doing it if this persuasion fails), and the weakest that of being authorised to request someone to carry out a task (who may legitimately refuse to do it). Another issue of authority relates to the setting of the limits within which a task has to be performed. The stronger degree of authority is that of deciding the limits within which another works, and the weaker that of recommending given limits but leaving the decision to the other person.

In relation to sanctions which can be exercised towards others, there are two major elements of authority. The first involves appraising the competence of others. The second element embraces their rewards, such as remuneration, career movements and position in the system (including possible dismissal). For both elements there are two degrees of authority: making a decision, or making a recommendation to the others' manager(s).

Prescribing relationships

Since doctors are accountable for ensuring an adequate quality of diagnosis and treatment for their patients, they have the authority to prescribe treatment which must be carried out by nursing and other hospital staff at specified times. Not only do doctors set such limits but they also monitor adherence to them, and appraise the quality of the work performed in pursuance of their prescriptions (i.e. the tasks they have initiated). Inevitably this leads to the appraisal of the competence of the person performing the work, such as a nurse or physiotherapist working under another professional manager, to whom a doctor may make a recommendation as to whether the performer should be rewarded or reprimanded. If the doctor judged that the performance was below the minimum acceptable standard, then the matter might be taken up with his own superior for the latter to discuss with a more senior person in the other profession. Often professional staff are in such prescribing relationships. These become the more common as organisations make increasing use of consulting firms to advise and support parts of their activities.

Attachments

The process of attachment commonly occurs with a group of technical or professional and specialist practitioners, who are managed by a fellow professional, and who are assigned to work for other persons or departments. Their professional head retains accountability and authority for them, but the person to whom an individual is attached is accountable for assigning work to him. The person to whom the attachment is made can veto the appointment if it is felt that the attached individual would not provide a satisfactory service, or can ask for any attached persons to be transferred if they appear to be performing work below minimum acceptable standards.

A variation of the attachment relationship occurs in organisations where the same specialism (or 'function') provides expertise at two levels, for example in the area of accountancy at head office and subsidiary level. At head office, the managing director has reporting to him the chief accountant, who is held accountable for the professional competence of any other accountant recruited as a subordinate to the general manager of any subsidiary. Equally, the general manager is held accountable for the performance of the subsidiary, so he in turn depends upon the subordinate accountant to provide him with information, analyses and recommendations which enable him to run the subsidiary efficiently. Consequently, the chief accountant and the general manager of the subsidiary share in the selection and appraisal of the subordinate, who in practice has two 'bosses'. Such relationships are best made explicit in writing, any difficulties being resolved by the managing director. The arrangement is typical of so-called 'functional' organisations where decentralisation is being introduced. This leads towards 'matrix organisations' (see Chapter 4).

Staff specialist relationships

In co-ordinating the work of subordinates, a manager in a large enterprise may need specialised assistance in the day-to-day planning of the work of subordinates, in controlling their activities, or in overcoming technical difficulties encountered, say, with materials, equipment or processes. Whereas a supervisor deals with many aspects of the work of the manager's subordinates, the staff specialist concentrates on only one aspect of work.

We can illustrate the relationship in the work of a planner and programmer (for example, a production planner). This person is accountable for preparing sound and co-ordinated plans, and issuing clear instructions at an appropriate time. (Another person may be accountable for checking progress in accordance with such plans.) These plans and instructions are conceived within the policies set by the manager, so that the planner in fact gives orders. But the planner cannot insist upon the orders being carried out. If the manager's subordinates feel that the plans are unrealistic or that they cannot comply with the instructions for good reasons, then they may raise the matter with the manager. Equally, the planner may report difficulties in getting agreement but cannot report on the competence of the manager's subordinates or their performance. (A planner should obviously consult the subordinates before planning.)

Monitoring and co-ordinating roles

A person in a monitoring role is accountable for checking that the activities of members of the organisation conform to adequate standards, and for doing their utmost to persuade them to modify their performance to meet those standards. Typically, such monitoring is exemplified by adherence to regulations, levels of expenditure, technical standards of work, or progress on a specific project. The monitor has to have the authority to secure first-hand knowledge of the monitored person's activities and problems. But if the monitor is dissatisfied with the outcome of his persuasive efforts, then a report has to be made to the monitored person's manager who must then investigate the matter. Inspection is a typical monitoring function, except that the inspector does not initiate tasks.

In a co-ordinating role, the person concerned is accountable for co-ordinating the activities of others within the framework of some defined task, the definition of which is acceptable to all those concerned. Such activities might include the production of a plan or a report, the implementation of a project or finding a solution to an unexpected operational problem. In relation to the task, the co-ordinator monitors progress, helps to overcome problems, and establishes and maintains co-ordinated work programmes. The co-ordinator has authority to propose action, arrange meetings and check progress, but those co-ordinated have the right, in a situation of disagreement, to go direct to those who set the tasks to be co-ordinated. The co-ordinator does not assess the performance of those being co-ordinated, and can only persuade people what should be done. Typically a major change programme will often be overseen by a steering group, the chairman of which might be responsible for co-ordinating the activities of the departments involved.

Service-giving and scanning relationships

Characteristically, large modern enterprises provide a wide range of services to their employees to enable them to do their work. Typing, copying, purchasing and maintenance are typical examples. Those giving service have accountability for providing it to authorised people, who may request the services they need. If the service-giver cannot comply with the request, this must be stated, giving reasons why, and indicating when the service will be available. If the delay prevents the service-seeker from completing a task on time, his authority is limited to reporting the fact to his manager, leaving the latter to decide what further should be done. In a scanning relationship, the individual's accountability is usually for gathering, processing or presenting data, the only authority being to report the information to prescribed persons without comment or interpretation.

Prescribed and discretionary activities

So far we have concentrated mainly on tasks assigned by a manager to a subordinate, or tasks which represent a response by the subordinate to a request or to an initiative from a person elsewhere. Initiative, however, has been rarely mentioned, except when alluding to the giving of advice.

Elliott Jacques (1976) notes that the essence is 'to carry out tasks and achieve outputs within target completion times, within expense and quality limits, and conforming to such prescribed methods and procedures as have been fixed as a matter of policy'. But he continues later:

The work, however, in carrying out a task consists not in conforming to the prescribed limits but in deciding how within those limits to carry out the task. . . . The work is what is left to the person to use his own discretion to do. If there is no discretion or judgement to be used in carrying out a task, then the task can be done by an automatic machine tool.

Experience suggests that employees (even managers) vary considerably in the extent to which an individual exercises discretion or demonstrates initiative. We can exemplify the exercise of discretion by the judgement used by a sales representative in deciding when and how to approach a client; or by a typist in laying out a page; or by a researcher noting unusual results; or by a chief executive in deciding resource allocations.

Demands, constraints and choices

Rosemary Stewart (1982) has analysed the work of managers under three categories: demands; constraints; and choices. 'Demands' refers to what any manager must do; 'constraints' covers the factors, internal or external to the organisation, that limit what the manager can do; 'choices' refers to activities that the manager can, but does not have to, do, so that he has opportunities to do different work, and in different ways, from another manager.

Amongst the common constraints limiting managerial choice are those of resources, such as buildings; legal and trade-union constraints; the limitations of equipment; physical location; the attitudes of other people; and organisational policies and procedures, such as the constraints imposed upon a manager by the definition of the work to be done by his unit (such as that of a melting shop in a steelworks).

However, Rosemary Stewart, using the term 'domain' to refer to a unit's area of operation, suggests that some domains offer scope for choice where the output is not clearly prescribed. More scope perhaps exists in staff and service jobs, in some sales jobs, and in some branch or subsidiary management posts, as well as in the advisory jobs to which we referred earlier. (Indeed, another choice for managers is to develop expertise in a field neglected by others.) Amongst jobs offering a choice of domain are those of corporate planning manager, personnel manager, safety manager, maintenance engineering and management accounting.

Another approach to choice involves work-sharing between a manager and subordinates, where the latter are knowledgeable and skilled. This may happen in the marketing function when the senior manager has frequently to travel abroad and others deputise in his absence. In management teams there is also scope for individuals to play roles beyond those of their functional expertise, such as leading a special project team.

We have examined at some length the constraints which an organisation imposes upon its managers and their subordinates as the logical consequence of relating the authority of individuals to their accountability. We have seen how the objects of an enterprise and the operational activities chosen by its management to achieve those objects affect the nature of the tasks given to managers and their subordinates, and to those who provide activities supporting them, and of course the accountabilities of those concerned. Despite the emphasis upon the prescription of behaviour appropriate to given accountabilities, we have also tried to point to areas of choice where the manager can express his individuality in the exercise of discretion and initiative.

Case study: A review of the role of supervisors in a process plant company

This case study deals with a review of the role of supervisors in what has been, since 1956, a medium-sized process plant company in the north-west of England. Working within the petroleum industry, the company was very profitable until stiffer competition led to a reduction in market share from 1973 onwards (combined, of course, with the impact of oil-price increases). Since 1979 major reorganisations, productivity improvements and redundancy schemes have led to dramatic improvements in productivity (140 per cent in the period 1981–3).

Typically supervisors/foremen work in a fragmented, fluid and sometimes pressured situation. This flows in part from the unpredictability of the production process, in part from the often diverse nature of the tasks and responsibilities they work with today. Many supervisors/foremen must react quickly to problems on or related to the plant. This is encouraged by the management through a conscious policy of decentralisation, given impetus by the reductions in manpower which have been effected and which necessarily place more demands on people throughout the structure. There is, in any event, a logic to it. As many people said, out of hours (at night when the foreman is the senior member of the management team on the site) the foreman *is* the company – and out of hours is the majority of the week! Coherence between 'out of hours' and normal working is to be encouraged but not formalised.

Changes to manpower levels have left small teams ('without much padding'), with the need for good teamwork, co-ordination and co-operation. The key words here are self-esteem, mutual confidence and trust. The supervisor needs to be confident of management support and backing – and where once this was lacking, it has now become an important part of management style.

Change erodes self-esteem, which must then be rebuilt. Good teamworking skills are based upon the confidence which grows from self-esteem. To feel he can motivate and control others, he needs to believe in himself and his own abilities. This comes partly from management style, as already discussed, partly from the ability to understand and improve one's own position and performance. The latter demands personal access to the relevant information. He needs to know where things are going wrong and to have the freedom to put them right. Ultimately there may be a case for regular feedback and appraisal from the manager – initially the impetus must come from within. Self-management, self-control and self-confidence come from within, they are not a gift from others. As we shall see, a number of practical ideas have emerged which would allow these ideas to be given effect.

Developing the role of the supervisor implies the need to develop the role of the men they supervise. There seem to be opportunities here in many areas. Significant changes to working practices have been achieved in recent years. Flexibility has been practised on the site by what seems, by general agreement, to be a co-operative and pragmatic workforce. In some areas efforts to involve the workforce and to work towards achieving better understanding have led to a constructive response.

A summary is now given of the demands, constraints and choices in the supervisor's job following the analytical scheme presented by Stewart (1982). The data were collected through in-depth interviews with nine supervisors. The demands on the supervisor are as follows:

1. Looking after people and dealing with day-to-day problems.
2. Liaison with other departments.
3. Applying a series of predetermined rules and conditions.
4. Assigning tasks.
5. Monitoring performance, quantity control, and machine utilisation.
6. 'Out of hours' responsibility.
7. Direct involvement in departmental work.
8. Training and supporting staff.

Overall, then, it is a highly fragmented job with some interdependence with staff from other departments. The constraints which apply are as follows:

1. Targets, specifications, operating conditions and schedules.
2. Unpredictability of process.
3. Resources, particularly manpower.
4. Financial, placing limits on implementation of improvement ideas.

5. Knowledge: technical (technical knowledge of plant limited and information support poor – tends to be 'after the fact'); financial (limited understanding of budgets and budget system, costs and trends), and personnel, wage agreements.
6. Labour flexibility, specific problems.
7. Attitudes, men wary of change who do not expect them to manage.

The choices available are as follows:

1. Technical decision-making within the bounds of predetermined rules.
2. Judgement and experience used to interpret problem situations.
3. Technical back-up available.
4. Crucial role in achieving change through monitoring agreements.
5. Innovation and improvements, an important aspect of the problem-solving element of the job.
6. Monitoring employee performance, providing support.
7. Technical decision-making, important in maintenance.

In Figure 2.1 we present a fuller analysis of these jobs.

As the supervisors view it, their job makes high demands on them in various areas. Relationships with other departments are important, thus highly developed boundary management skills are required. Supervisory skills are important on what is a complex and demanding plant. Skills with the 'boss' and peers are important and teamwork is crucial, the latter because the plant is spread over many hundreds of yards – one round of all the control points means a walk several miles. Finally, 'exposure' is vital. If something goes wrong, it is highly visible on this process plant.

Perhaps one interesting point to emerge from the analysis so far relates to the constraints which apply. These do not all come from senior management or the organisation structure. Peers, other departments and the attitudes of subordinates all present constraints. Thus it is that whilst constraints come from many sources they are not immutable.

This analysis brought forth a number of ideas. Supervisors were judged to be technically very effective. Their personal and managerial effectiveness was less developed. No formal or systematic appraisal system existed. It was recognised that supervisors should be involved in reviewing shift performance. More importantly, developments in the management information system were in hand. The supervisors were to be involved in this work. Assessment and training were needed as was fuller and more effective information on company plans. A more effective and co-operative management style was needed to support supervisors. These and other ideas

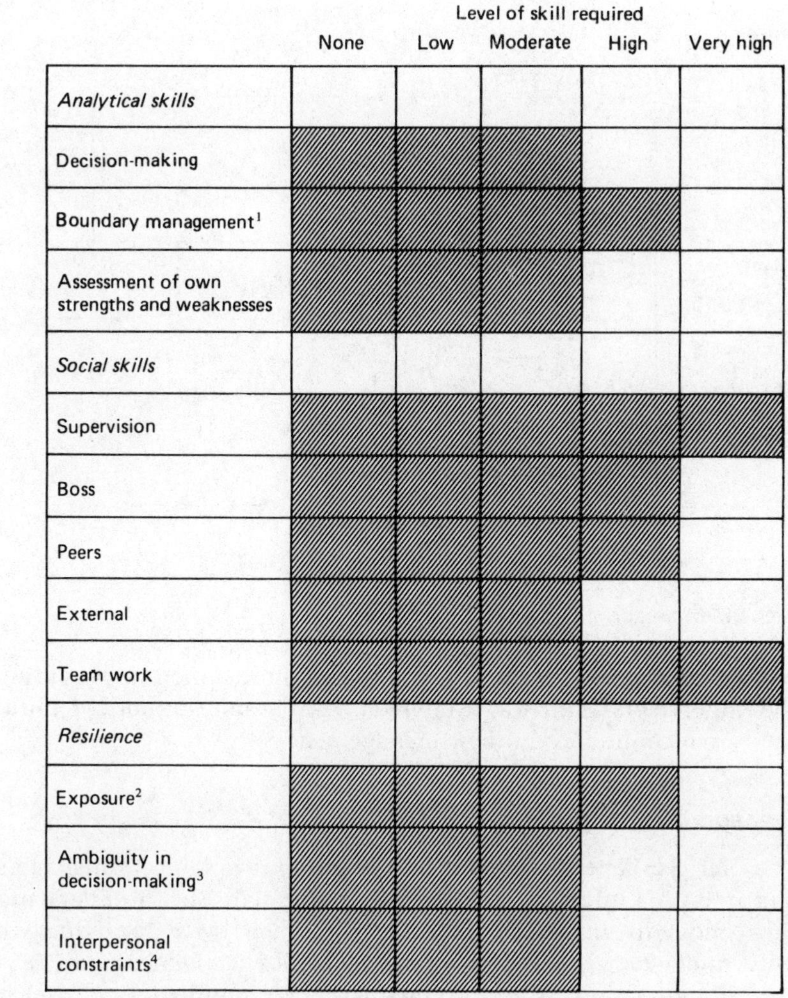

Level of skill required

	None	Low	Moderate	High	Very high
Analytical skills					
Decision-making	▨	▨	▨		
Boundary management[1]	▨	▨	▨	▨	
Assessment of own strengths and weaknesses	▨	▨	▨		
Social skills					
Supervision	▨	▨	▨	▨	▨
Boss	▨	▨	▨	▨	
Peers	▨	▨	▨	▨	
External	▨	▨	▨	▨	
Team work	▨	▨	▨	▨	▨
Resilience					
Exposure[2]	▨	▨	▨	▨	
Ambiguity in decision-making[3]	▨	▨	▨		
Interpersonal constraints[4]	▨	▨	▨		

Note: Modal value shown 'hatched'.

[1] Boundary management refers to the skills of managing the interface between departments where problems occur involving more than one department and the skills of managing the relationship with external groups (local people, suppliers, contractors, etc.), particularly 'out of hours'.

[2] Exposure refers to the extent to which the consequences of errors or poor performance are both immediately obvious and costly.

[3] Ambiguity refers to the degree of uncertainty in decision-making, regarding both means and ends.

[4] Interpersonal constraints refers to the extent to which the exercise of the job is influenced by the activities/expectations of people from other departments.

Fig. 2.1 The supervisor's job analysed.

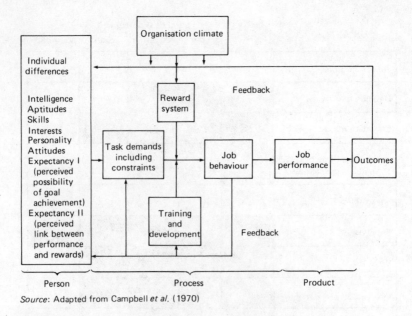

Fig. 2.2 Managerial effectiveness.

formed the basis of a longer-term programme aimed at providing the supervisors with the knowledge skills and support to build their own confidence in their management role.

Managerial effectiveness

Thus far we have considered the discretion available to managers and how this might be analysed and explored. But to understand how and why managers might explore their own discretion we must understand something of management effectiveness and managerial motivation. Much of this will be examined in the next chapter. At this stage in the discussion, a simple model of managerial effectiveness is presented in Fig. 2.2.

The important variables are related in the model as shown. Feedback from effective managerial performance will influence expectancies and, therefore, in a supportive organisation, climate may lead to further improvement.

Managerial effectiveness is a function of personal and organisational factors. The skills, attitudes and preferences of the individual are important. But so are the opportunities, training, development and support provided by the organisation. In the case study the ideas for change focused upon the training, development and support available to the supervisors. In the next chapter managerial motivation will be examined in greater detail. This will be linked directly to managerial effectiveness and the manager's career development.

Concluding comment

This chapter has examined the key issue of managerial accountability and discretion and choice in managerial jobs. It has been observed that accountability is a key emphasis in modern views on management. Ideas were reviewed on how to define and analyse managerial accountability. In the case study this was taken further by considering a specific job in these terms and looking at the development issues thus raised. The chapter ended by considering the question of managerial effectiveness. It is this issue, and the related ones of managerial motivation, career development and management development, which are now addressed.

Chapter 3

Manager motivation and development

Organisation structures

The design of organisation structures to suit the needs of the particular business enterprise or organisation, providing for the co-ordination of the diverse activities carried out within the enterprise or organisation, but also providing for adaptability to respond to changing circumstances, presents a challenge to management whose importance cannot be overstated. How an organisation is structured affects the pursuit of objectives and the implementation of plans. People and resources are allocated to the tasks which must be performed, and co-ordination is provided. Working methods, rules and procedures define the ways in which tasks are to be performed and/or establish criteria for task performance, output or quality. These are typically all related to reward systems, planning and scheduling systems, and monitoring systems. The aspects of the structure of an organisation are articulated in the information system.

Moreover, the structure of the organisation provides a decision-support system. Arrangements are made for the collection and processing of information relevant to the decisions managers make. Specialist posts are often created to provide for such arrangements. Accountants and organisation and methods personnel will, for example, collect and process information on various aspects of the performance of the organisation. This information will be evaluated and presented to decision-makers either regularly (to a senior management meeting) or in response to particular circumstances (for example, when a major contract becomes open for bids). The tasks of the organisation create a need for decisions to be made. In practice decision-makers decide that certain tasks will be undertaken and others not, from the range of tasks which could be undertaken and for which a market exists. For a decision system to be effective, provision for monitoring trends in the market is essential. Changes in technology, in resource markets for capital or labour, and in the product market, will affect the performance of any organisation requiring adaptation.

Following Child (1984), the main dimensions of an organisation structure are as follows:

1. The allocation of tasks and responsibilities, providing appropriate discretion over methods and use of resources.
2. The designation of formal reporting relationships, determining spans of control of managers and supervisors.
3. The grouping of individuals into sections and departments, and the grouping of departments into divisions or other major units.
4. The delegation of authority with associated procedures for performance monitoring and evaluation, which may either be regular or operate by exception.
5. The design of communication and co-ordinating systems, to provide information and participation in decision-making.
6. The provision of reward systems to motivate individuals.
7. The establishment of decision-support systems such as regular management meetings, project teams and specialist posts or departments.

Where the structure of an organisation is inappropriate or deficient we would expect to see a number of possible problems emerging, including the following:

1. Low motivation and morale of employees.
2. Delayed or poor decisions.
3. Conflict between departments.
4. Rising costs.
5. A tendency to stick to the rules and regulations, whether or not appropriate action will follow.
6. Lack of capacity to adapt to changing circumstances.

If we observe problems such as those listed here (and this is not meant as an exhaustive list), then we have reason to conclude that the structure of the organisation is deficient in some way. It is important to recognise that the dimensions of an organisation structure can be designed in different ways and they may vary considerably in practice.

The organisation form with which we are all most familiar is bureaucracy. Bureaucratic structures are characterised by a high degree of job specialisation, by reliance on formal procedures and paperwork, by hierarchy, by clear and significant status differentials, and by an emphasis on control. Bureaucratic structures are intended to provide for equal treatment for all employees; a reliance upon the expertise, skills and experience relevant to the job; specific standards of work and output; the maintenance of records and files dealing with work and output; the setting up and enforcement of rules and regulations that serve the interests of the organisation; and a recognition that rules and regulations are binding upon managers as well as on other employees.

However, in environments which are changing rapidly, rules, regulations and working procedures can quickly become out of date and irrelevant. Moreover, rules and regulations can become barriers behind which individual managers hide or which they use to justify incorrect decisions. Inflexible systems of procedure can create de-motivating conditions for employees and can reduce the ability of managers or employees to innovate. From this we could conclude that a bureaucratic structure might be suitable for an organisation dealing with a stable and simple environment. Conversely, an altogether more flexible and innovative structure would be suitable for a changing, complex environment.

Contingency theory is a label applied to a body of recent work based on the assumption that there is 'no one best way' to design an organisation structure; the effectiveness of the design of a particular organisation is contingent upon various factors, normally stated to include the technology, the environment, the history of the organisation, norms and expectations, and the size of the organisation. Lawrence and Lorsch (1967) were the first to use the term 'contingency theory' as a convenient way of describing this empirical view of organisation structures and process. However, the earlier work of Burns and Stalker (1961) and Woodward (1965) are important applications of the approach.

Exponents of contingency theories have advocated a shift in the approach of organisation designers to the problem of organisation choice. Rather than propose one strategy as being of universal application within organisations, contingency theorists have suggested that design, management and control strategies should be developed to meet the situation within which they are to be applied. The theory suggests that organisational performance depends on the extent to which the organisation secures a good match between situation and structure. Child (1984) summarises it as follows: contingency theory 'regards the design of an effective organisation as necessarily having to be adapted to cope with the "contingencies" which derive from the circumstances of environment, technology, scale, resources and other factors in the situation in which the organisation is operating'.

The components of organisation structure (for example, the degree of formalisation of procedures, centralisation of decision-making, number of levels in hierarchies, and the spans of control of managers) can take different forms. Lorsch (1970) suggests that 'structure of an organisation is not an immutable given, but rather a set of complex variables about which managers can exercise considerable choice'.

The contingency-theory approach to organisation design attempts to take account of all four components, uses the organisation as the unit of analysis, and tends to accept a managerial framework, particularly in respect of organisational purposes. By stating that the components of an organisation can be changed, they introduce the idea of choice; called 'strategic choice' by Galbraith (1977). For Galbraith, organisation design involves attempts to make the goals of organisation, the means applied and the people, 'coherent'. The phrase 'strategic choice' is used to emphasise the available choice of goals, means and processes for integrating individuals into the organisation and also the choice as to whether some or all of these goals, means and processes should be changed to meet changes in the environment. The remainder of this chapter discusses the question of how individuals, particularly managers, can be 'integrated' within the organisation. A more detailed discussion of organisation structures will be provided in Chapter 4.

Motivation

There is a wide variety of views on the subject of motivation and work. This section will attempt a broad overview of some of the current ideas and approaches to raising the awareness which managers need to maximise organisation effectiveness.

It has become increasingly recognised that there is no one guiding rule on how to motivate people. Human complexity is such that what may motivate in one set of situations or circumstances will not necessarily act in the same positive way in another. Therefore, in order to create motivation it is necessary to develop an awareness both of the organisation's needs and the needs of the individual within that organisation.

People work in order to satisfy direct needs, to gain a sense of personal worth and to feel a part of society. So why do we need to motivate people? Motivation urges an individual to do something, to achieve, to reach goals, thereby maximising a resource which will contribute to the organisation's success and to the individual's personal well-being.

Studying motivation in work situations is challenging because of its complexity. Work places vary in size, shape and form, and in what they produce; they serve a variety of types of customer in many different financial structures. But common elements do exist and understanding is important. Money, hierarchies and tasks are common characteristics of organisations. Some organisations motivate their employees by using pay incentives, some by offering stimulating jobs, others by democratic management (Lawler 1973). The essential feature to keep in mind is that each organisation will require varying factors to motivate its employees. For example, what is needed to motivate assembly-line workers will differ from what is needed to motivate a research team. What also needs to be taken into account is the individuality of each human being. Work is a central feature of life and people spend much of their waking hours working. What makes them satisfied with work differs from one person to another. Undoubtedly money is a primary incentive but through work people also gain companionship, self-esteem and a sense of worth. The absence of one or more of these will affect attitudes towards work. Even with so many complex issues surrounding motivation, it is still worthwhile trying to understand it. Understanding motivation helps predict how individuals react and respond to organisational situations. Predictability improves accuracy and subsequently this can enable managers to create a climate which will encourage motivation.

Equity theory

People see what is happening to others around them and draw comparisons with their own situation. If they see themselves as getting more or less than others around them then they feel uneasy because their sense of fairness is violated. Dissatisfaction will result if they perceive that they are not being treated fairly in comparison with others. Adams (1963; 1965) looked at the effects of wage inequity on work practices and found that it was not the actual level of pay an individual receives for his efforts that influences his behaviour; rather it is what he receives *in relation to* others in similar situations which is the influencing factor. If his pay falls below that which others doing similar work receive, then he will see this as unfair and in response adjust his productivity to what he perceives as an appropriate level. Overpayment, according to Adam's research, is seen as less attractive than equitable payment, and so equity affects the attractiveness of rewards. How the individual perceives the balance of contribution and reward is the central feature of equity theory.

Achievement

The need to achieve has been identified as a motivator. McClelland (1951; 1961) describes the need to achieve as a desire to strive for excellence or to be successful in competitive situations. He believes that a level of achievement motivation is apparent in most individuals but that the extent of its importance is dependent on many factors and influenced by early childhood experiences. For example, children from families which placed a high priority on independence and performance throughout early formative childhood will exhibit a high need achievement and this is rewarded and reinforced by parents. The research identifies that achievement motivation can be an appropriate stimulus in some organisations. Where tasks are routine and repetitive and competition is absent, achievement motivation is not likely to work. In situations where challenge and competition are evident then achievement motivation can act as a positive motivator. McClelland further suggests that those who have a high achievement need will seek out work situations where this can be satisfied and tend to be successful where a high level of performance is needed.

Self-actualisation

The need for work to be satisfying and rewarding has led some psychologists to study the importance of human needs in relation to work. The research of Abraham Maslow (1954) has generated much interest in motivation within organisations. Maslow puts forward the idea that human needs can be expressed in a hierarchical model, and that motivation springs from needs which are not satisfied. Maslow believes that individuals have a need to grow and develop, which he describes as 'self-actualisation'. By using and developing their capacities people being to self-actualise; they experience satisfaction and enjoyment. These feelings are intrinsic; the reward is in how they feel about themselves. People strive to fulfil basic needs. Self-actualisers, once these basic needs are fulfilled, then develop a need to grow, express themselves, release their full capacity. Once need is satisfied then it is replaced by another; growth creates more growth (Lawler 1973). Therefore self-actualising differs from primary drives for the opposite reason; for example, if we are hungry we satisfy this by eating, then the need is fulfilled.

Maslow then applies this concept to motivation in organisations. Managers in particular have a high desire to self-actualise as they seek challenge and exhibit a high desire for promotion (Porter

1964). Large organisations provide career opportunities through career development plans and training. These not only contribute to promotion possibilities, but can also satisfy needs for self-development.

It is interesting to note that Maslow's self-actualising motivator is an intrinsic desire and not directly related to reward systems such as money or status. It is clear that these rewards are synonymous with promotion but they become ends not means.

According to Maslow's model, as basic needs are satisfied, personal development becomes more central. His model identifies five levels of human needs:

Physiological – the need for food and basic comfort.

Safety – security; freedom from pain or illness.

Love – the need for affection and sense of belonging.

Esteem – the need for respect and recognition; an intrinsic sense of achievement.

Self-actualisation – the realisation of self-fulfillment; recognition of potential.

According to Maslow, once lower-level needs are satisfied, their importance decreases and people are motivated to satisfy a higher-level need. This process continues towards achieving self-actualisation.

Others have modified Maslow's original notion of need hierarchy. Alderfer (1969), whilst in basic agreement with Maslow, has refined the satisfaction of needs to three factors: *existence* (safety and security); *relatedness* (love and affiliation); *growth* (esteem and self-actualisation). Whilst Alderfer agrees with Maslow that growth needs are important, he believes that the absence of satisfaction of higher-level needs tends to lead to lower-level needs becoming more important. Alderfer also assumes that all needs can be active at the same time.

The hierarchy of needs has had an important impact upon organisational psychology as it provides a powerful instrument in predicting the outcome of responses by the individual on the part of the organisation. It implies that as people progress within an organisation their lower-level needs are satisfied and they strive towards growth and self-actualisation. Conversely, it implies that when people feel threatened, job security is at risk and then maintaining basic needs becomes predominantly important. When an organisation provides needs which are valued by the individual they want more. As lower-level needs such as good working conditions, higher pay and security are satisfied, higher-level needs such as interesting work, opportunities for decision-making, and so on, will become necessary.

The ideas of Maslow and others led to substantial interest in motivation in the 1940s and 1950s. The theoretical impetus was linked to the practical impetus from the need to generate increased productivity in manufacturing during the period 1940 onwards (this was due to many reasons – rearmament, war, competition, mechanisation and so on). Thus many empirical studies were carried out. Herzberg and others completed a detailed review of this literature in 1958. Later on he was involved in developing a two-factor theory in motivation.

Two-factor theory

The two-factor theory (see Table 3.1), developed by Herzberg *et al.* (1959) and Herzberg (1966) distinguished some factors of work as satisfying from others as dissatisfying. He found that job satisfaction and dissatisfaction were two separate, independent factors; not bipolar extremities, but unipolar, operating at the same time. He suggests that different parts of the job will influence feelings of satisfaction and dissatisfaction. Therefore, a person can feel satisfied, e.g. motivated, and dissatisfied at the same time. The only way satisfaction can be improved is by influencing the factors shown in Table 3.1. Examination of the two types of factors, however, does raise difficulties. Hygiene factors relate to inadequacies in either other people's jobs or the work environment, whereas motivators relate to self and/or one's own success. Consequently, criticism has been levelled at Herzberg's theory. However, self-actualisation and the two-factor theory enable us to distinguish intrinsically motivating features, and therefore have influence on job design and concern for worker satisfaction. Hellreigel *et al.* (1986) present a useful combination of these ideas, which we present in slightly modified form as Fig. 3.1.

Expectancy theory

Expectancy theory (Vroom 1964) looks at both individual and

Table 3.1. The two factor theory.

Motivators	Hygiene
(Satisfaction)	(Dissatisfaction)
Achievement	Company policy
Recognition	Supervision
Work itself	Salary
Responsibility	Interpersonal relations
Advancement	Working conditions

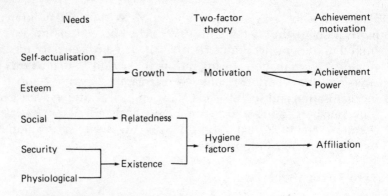

Fig. 3.1 A summary of some motivation theories.

environmental factors in order to explain motivation. Individuals are assumed to make decisions about how much to produce, quality, and so on. They are also assumed to have different needs and to seek different outcomes from work (job security, high pay, satisfying work). In addition, it is assumed that these choices will depend upon their perceptions of the likelihood that a particular behaviour (say, working hard) will lead to a desired outcome (high pay). Testing this model presents major difficulties to research workers. Nevertheless, the theory does lead to some interesting questions for managers. Is it possible to identify the outcomes employees value? Is it possible to identify desirable performance in order to motivate managers? Is it possible to ensure that the performance desired is seen as achievable by these managers? But if they wish to have challenge in their jobs then the performance level must be both achievable and challenging. Is it possible to link the outcomes people require with the performance managers require? Finally, is it possible to ensure that all managers recognise the importance of people's perception in all of this? – after all it is what people perceive to be true that may drive their behaviour.

Managerial motivation

A number of generalisations may be made about managerial motivation. Managers seem to value esteem, autonomy and achievement rather than security or social needs. It seems that this finding applies when managers are compared with non-managers and high-performing managers are compared with low-performing managers. Very little is known about managers' reward preferences. Until the 1970s many US studies seemed to show that managers preferred salary to fringe benefits and that there was little evidence that money was an incentive (Haire *et al.* 1967). With the growth of fringe benefits, share-option schemes and managerial buyouts, one wonders about the relevance of these findings today. Motivation may be a function of the changing environment, with increased focus upon individualism and accountability (see Chapter 1). So much has changed in the context of and nature of managerial work that one must conclude that management motivation is rather imperfectly understood.

However, though the body of knowledge of managerial motivation is limited, there is presently much concern with manager and management development. Management development is about the development of the tasks, purposes and objectives of management in an organisation. Manager development is linked to this but comprises those activities aimed at developing the individual manager. Just as there is a need to pay attention to the integration of the individual into the organisation so there is a need to integrate manager and management development. They do not integrate automatically.

The key means of integrating manager and management development is effective organisational learning. If more effective means of management can be developed, then systems and processes through which people learn will follow. Organisational learning (Argyris, 1982; 1985) involves the detection and correction of error. In *single-loop learning* an error is detected and corrected in a way which enables the organisation to carry on with current policies and objectives. This mode of learning, then, acts like a thermostat. In *double-loop learning*, on the other hand, when an error is detected, its correction involves the modification of organisational policies and objectives.

Organisations usually cope with single-loop learning but have problems with double-loop. This is because, as long as the original objective is maintained, there is no problem, but if it is recognised that the original objective was wrong, problems arise because established organisational norms are violated. Questions of loyalty to the organisation are raised – who is going to tell the emperor he has no clothes on? Usually a series of tactical moves is necessary if pieces of information are gradually released in a way which is non-threatening both to senior management, who will be sensitive to criticism, and middle management, who need to be careful not to antagonise their superiors. Information must be conveyed, but how this is done without violating organisational norms and policies becomes a complex issue. Games need to be played which tease out the realities in a relatively harmless way so that participants can feel safe. Argyris believes organisations 'tend to create learning systems that inhibit double loop learning that calls into question their norms, objectives and basic policies' (Argyris and Schon 1978).

Membership of organisations

The individual within an organisation builds an image or representation of what that organisation is. His image is always incomplete and he will constantly try to complete it in order to put himself within the context of the organisation, to describe himself, to assess performance. He constantly matches himself with the organisation to find a comfortable 'fit'. He interacts with other members of the organisation, and with them constructs mutual descriptions which guide him through the organisation and indicate future actions. He constantly modifies these images about the organisation and also brings changes through himself to it. Changes within organisations will initiate new patterns which may conflict with its norms and individuals serve as agents of change within organisations. Shared images will either confirm or conflict, leading members modifying their images to re-establish expectations or adjust actions to regain congruence.

Impact of motivation on work

The way jobs are designed can have a positive effect upon feelings of satisfaction, performance and motivation. The combination of intrinsic and extrinsic rewards through work leads to satisfaction of needs, self-esteem, a sense of achievement. These then develop into effort and performance. How jobs are designed in order to maximise this potential and performance, is the subject of this section.

The scientific management approach developed by Taylor (1911) is now considered the traditional approach. Taylorism sees man as self-seeking; the worker is only interested in gaining reward. This attitude in turn requires that workers need close supervision and clearly planned tasks in order to achieve maximum efficiency.

Assembly-line production is characteristic of this approach. Its continued popularity is due to the belief that it has financial and engineering advantages. Virtually no training is necessary for assembly-line work, which, from an economic standpoint, makes it attractive. The limited skill required by workers means there is a constant flow of labour available to the company. Assembly-line work needs a high degree of mechanisation, requiring minimum physical effort. The standardised nature of the work maintains quality and output control. Each person on the line completes one part of the process. All this should in theory lead to a predictable, cost-effective, standardised product. The operation is overseen by a supervisor who can quickly assess the process and tell whether it is working efficiently. However, in many instances, this principle of scientific management is not without problems. Human beings simply do not always behave as we think they will! Staff turnover is epidemic where such processes are employed, with some companies showing staff turnover of over 100 per cent (Lawler 1973). With such a high degree of turnover the notion of cost-effectiveness is no longer tenable. Even though low-level skill is required, high rates of turnover will have a significant impact on recruitment resources. Absenteeism can be very high, due to the tedious nature of the work, and costly on grounds of both sickness benefit and the pool of labour required to keep the line running efficiently.

The Hawthorne Experiments (see Roethlisberger and Dickinson 1939) led to a forceful challenge to the scientific management approach. The individual is now seen as an active, social being responding to stimuli from the social structure, and adjusting his behaviour according to his individual interests and needs. The underlying belief is that workers produce better when they find the task interesting, when the work place provides social contact and when the workers are engaged in mutual help. An informal structure will have a positive effect on control, sanctions and, ultimately, productivity. The output of workers in a given organisation is controlled by the set of norms and behaviours adopted by them as a group. Man at work is no longer seen as a mere extension of his machine.

This has led to a restructuring of work practices in some organisations through a recognition of workers' social and psychological needs. If workers feel a part of the work practice their performance and output increase as long as there is congruence between the organisation's expectations and those of the group.

The 'humanising' of the work place has been shown to reduce absenteeism, reduce turnover and increase output. Job design can be planned in ways which incorporate human needs so as to produce high satisfaction for the individual and greater productivity for the organisation. Tavsky and Parke (1976) define work design as in terms of *job rotation*, where the worker moves from one job station to another every few hours or days; *job enlargement*, where tasks are grouped together so as to provide him with variety; and *job enrichment*, where tasks provide him variety, complexity and opportunities to use his discretion.

Job enrichment and job enlargement have been seen by many social scientists to have an impact on motivation. Job enrichment and job enlargement stimulate challenge and interest. Job enlargement, sometimes referred to as *horizontal expansion*, gives the worker a variety of tasks, while job enrichment, sometimes referred to as *vertical expansion*, is more concerned with increasing autonomy and gives the worker greater responsibility. Writers in the main seem in agreement that a combination of both is likely to produce increased motivation, which in turn leads to higher productivity. Training is larger and obviously more costly and a higher skill level is demanded which in turn means higher remuneration. There are many studies which look at the effects of such work design; most indicate a higher level of productivity. Lawler (1973) gives the example of a study by Kunloff (1966):

An electronics firm that manufactures measuring instruments on an assembly line was experiencing work quality, turnover, absenteeism and productivity-flexibility problems. To solve these problems the firm enriched the jobs of the assembly line workers. Instead of assembling only one part of the instrument, each worker had to assemble a whole instrument. In many cases this represented a week's work for one employee. When the employee finished the instrument, he tested it, signed it and sent it to the customer. If any problems developed with the instrument, the worker was personally responsible for correcting it.

The immediate effect of the programme was a fall in productivity and quality. This could be attributed to new learning skills being developed in order to cope with assembling the whole instrument rather than just part of it. Six months later productivity returned to its former rate and quality increased. Absenteeism and turnover both decreased and workers experienced a higher level of job satisfaction.

So, to summarise, the way work is arranged can provide opportunities for individuals to experience greater satisfaction. How this is done depends upon the type of job and organisation, as indicated earlier, and the design of the job is a crucial variable in determining the types of reward it supplies.

Career planning and development

The concept of career involves much more than simply looking at promotion opportunities. It also covers the experience of the individual within the organisation and how he responds to this. Seeking opportunities to change and/or widen work experience, gain higher status, increase job satisfaction and improve working conditions are all events linked with career development.

Career satisfaction is dependent on the value the individual places upon work within the context of out-of-work interests. His background and life experiences will affect the opportunities he values and seeks. Super (1957) explains that career issues vary according to life stages. He describes these stages as follows:

Crystallisation (14–18 years). The individual formulates ideas about what work means and what kind of work would be appropriate. This requires the development of both occupational and self-concepts which mediate career choices.

Specification (18–21 years). At this stage career direction is narrowed down to more specific areas and steps are taken through education and training to activate these ideas.

Implementation (21–24 years). At this stage a career preference is implemented. The individual seeks out relevant job opportunities and identifies further training needs. There is a strong desire to plan.

Stabilisation (25–35 years). The individual settles down within a specific job area and seeks to demonstrate the talents appropriate to promote career choice.

Consolidation (30–mid-40s). Now the individual has become established and has practised and developed the skills required by the job.

It is clear that Super does not view career moves as isolated events. They are to be considered within the context of individual life experiences. As the individual moves through life stages, different vocational behaviours are appropriate. Out-of-work interests, the nature of the organisation, family and social ties will all affect career decisions. For Super, vocational maturity is reached when job expectations match the organisation's character and can be comfortably fitted into the context of the individual's overall lifestyle.

Career development requires planning in order that it may be successful. Many authors (London and Strumpf 1982; Super 1980) believe that successful career planning can be achieved by goal-setting. Goals need to be expressed in terms of both long- and short-term needs; where a career will ultimately lead and how to maximise opportunities in order to get there. To facilitate this process several features are required: accurate self-assessment of the person we are, our wants and needs, skill assessment and identification of personal and work-related strengths and weaknesses. An examination of the organisation will help to develop realistic and achievable goals and specify career direction through planning. Appropriate training is required to prepare for target positions and to maximise career potential.

Career development is a two-way process. It requires individual career management to be placed within the context of organisational factors.

Individual career management

According to London and Strumpf (1982) career progression is enhanced by task performance. This can be achieved by assessing skills, interests and potential work roles, developing realistic career plans based on self-assessment and job opportunities within the organisation, seeking out necessary training to prepare for target positions. They suggest this process can be enhanced by clear, accurate views of one's skills and interests. This requires scrutiny of current positions; where you are and how you got there. This can be compounded by determining career goals and work role preferences.

Organisational factors

The organisation needs to define career progression by providing job opportunities and career paths associated with these. Personnel policies should be outlined and career opportunities offered to suitable candidates. Human resource management helps organisations to facilitate these decisions. These systems should include planning future labour, both technical and managerial. A sound selection system targets for appropriate employees who are likely to remain within the organisation for several years. Assessment and performance appraisals are to identify areas which require enhancing with the individual's potential and which can predict performance at higher levels.

The organisation needs to encourage regular self-assessment to complement career development; training and development opportunities to encourage movement through the organisation. Staff support is necessary to enable information to flow in a positive way so the individual is in touch with systems and policies. Encouragement to co-manage careers is also important as it provides opportunities to expand career potential.

Implications for the organisation

These suggestions have implications for the organisation. It needs to recognise movement of personnel, laterally and vertically through-out the organisation, to get maximum potential from employees and to benefit the needs of the organisation; selecting the most suitably qualified personnel and providing challenging, interesting experiences. When an organisation is committed to career planning then it should form part of the career management process. This in turn should provide supervisors whose role is to take responsibility for the development of subordinates and help in their career decision-making. Managers need to design systems and provide policy on career management. 'Effective career management maintains a standard of excellence at all organisational levels. This is accomplished through the inter-related human resource functions of personnel planning, selection, assessment of performance and potential, career planning, training and development and staffing decisions' (London and Strumpf 1982).

Design for career planning

Often there are no formal paths between positions within organisations. However, several studies (Dalton, Thompson, and Price 1977) show that changes in assignments, when compatible with career stages, help in developing careers. Developing realistic career paths can be defined in three stages (London and Strumpf 1982; Walker 1976):
1. Defining work activities.
2. Identifying personal requirements.
3. Recognising job families.
Work activities can be described as job content and the description should reflect what employees do on the job and what managers believe is done on the job. Personal requirements such as skills training can then be identified on this basis. These skills can then be translated into job families – groups of jobs requiring similar transferable skills. This bank of experience can then provide movement in order to maximise career opportunities. Identification of career paths can then provide role models and help higher management select protégés. Identifying career paths is important for the individual. Through exposure to different tasks the individual will develop aptitudes though not have specific skills so job assignments will identify areas which the individual will want to maximise. So career paths need first to be identified and secondly tailored to fit the developmental needs of the individual. Career plans require a high degree of flexibility and experience on tasks which will produce both positive and negative feedback to the individual. This need

not invalidate the plan since this is the vehicle which is providing guidance and establishing realistic goals. As new information is realised, flexibility will allow this to be incorporated and thus provide continuity.

Career planning programmes

We need to begin by defining responsibilities. These fall into three basic categories; the organisation, the individual and shared responsibilities (London and Strumpf 1982).

Organisational responsibility

This is the need for the organisation to provide relevant career information to employees. This includes salary scales and company information – its economic position, job requirements and training opportunities.

Individual responsibility

The need for continuous self-assessment and overall career planning is largely the responsibility of the individual, though some organisations provide a seedbed for this process. These may be psychometric tests and assessment activities, feedback, life/career planning.

Shared responsibility

Here we can generally determine two basic differences. The 'person-centred' approach, which attempts to fit the needs of the individual with those of the organisation, and the 'manager-centred' approach, spotting potential high fliers who have attributes which primarily fit the organisation's needs. The 'person-centred' approach largely places responsibility upon the individual to find his own way through the organisation with the organisation providing pointers towards information and resources available. It is then up to the individual to recognise and maximise potential opportunities. A viable career management model requires accurate information about the organisation for the individual to make predictable decisions and a communication network which is effective between the organisation and the employee.

When responsibility is shared between the individual and the organisation then it can be translated into meaningful career action. What does shared responsibility imply? Adequate access to accurate information about the organisation, opportunities for counselling and coaching for task development backed up by relevant training activities to prepare employees for target jobs.

What the organisation needs to give the individual

Career counselling

Much emphasis has been placed on the importance of career counselling in this section. It is useful to examine this concept in more detail in order to recognise its significance in career development.

The word 'counselling' is one we are familiar with. It is not confined to the work of professionals, such as marriage counsellors. Friends, colleagues and family are all at some point in our lives counsellors; people who listen to what we have to say, who understand and respect our views. Counsellors in general help clients to explore their needs by interviewing, interpreting and feeding back information. This function is useful in career development. It provides the individual with the structure to discuss career aspirations and how these fit into life landscapes; to discuss strengths and weaknesses, not only those the individual perceives but those he perceives within the organisation. These activities can be mutually beneficial as they can clarify the individual's ideas and highlight what the organisation can consider providing in order to build a stronger team. This may appear time consuming and costly on the face of it. But human resources are a valuable commodity within the organisation and time spent maintaining and overhauling it can be viewed as good investment in the organisation's future. The result of meaningful counselling capitalises opportunities and activities which fit a specific organisational setting.

Coaching

Subordinates need appraisals from superiors in order to improve performance. Superiors are in a position to observe and evaluate the behaviour and current performance of subordinates within the organisation. It is their role to provide relevant coaching and by this we mean outlining career opportunities and providing the means to expand the subordinates' potential. This procedure requires substantial commitment from both parties in order to be successful. Management by objectives is an approach which integrates self-evaluation with goal setting and is seen to be an effective process (London and Strumpf 1982). Seminars and workshops can help individuals towards self-development if they are overseen by superiors with relevant experience. This technique can assess and improve skills training through a developmental approach which gives guidance for coaching through discussion and feedback.

Other activities

Other activities, either in-house or outside the organisation, can enhance career development programmes. Courses with a focus on particular issues such as decision-making, leadership, managing people, and so on, can help individuals supplement for weaknesses in performance and promote competence. Courses designed for developing self-awareness through interaction with others can be useful in facilitating openness through realistic discussions on career plans and helping individuals identify personal strengths and weaknesses.

Career planning for special problems is also an important area. Such programmes focus on issues concerning retirement, mid-career problems, and so on, and can reduce anxiety and help weakened self-esteem by providing support and shared experiences. Career planning should integrate several needs with activities. The activities obviously depend upon the purpose of the programme and should relate to career stage, ability, the needs of the organisation, function of the job. The needs will vary according to the individual and the emphasis the organisation puts on promoting specific potential and skill.

Career development and organisation

In many large organisations, career development has become part of corporate planning which enables individuals openly to assess career opportunities. Here, personnel plans are in action offering vacancies ahead of time and demonstrating promotion plans which are easily identifiable by employees. Such organisations offer a mixture of the elements described earlier in career planning programmes. Dangers can exist if employee development is offered without career development. This often becomes evident through training programmes when organisations treat them as 'cure-alls'. The value of training should not be underestimated though it needs to be recognised that training cannot bring everyone to the organisation's desired level of competence nor should it alone become the measure by which individuals succeed or fail within the organisation. Invariably, some will not be willing or able to develop despite how much training is given and the problem of carrying 'dead wood', those whose careers have little chance of growth, cannot be dealt with by using training processes alone. Organisations providing career development programmes cannot rely on promoting employee development, i.e. training, without providing career development and the environment to nurture improvement.

Career perception and organisations

Individuals carry with them a perception of career and, according to Kanawaty (1976), this can be distinguished by two mutually dependent features: external career – the norm defined by the organisation or society – for example, doctor or engineer; and internal career – the individual's own perception of progress along career paths. Problems can arise when the individual's perception of career is difficult to match with organisational career development norms. The organisation's career development programme may be designed in such a way that it cannot keep pace with the speed of advancement the individual requires to develop. Therefore timespan becomes an issue. Kanawaty (1976) urges that these differences need not be irreconcilable and suggests that career development programmes could offer stimulating activities which would enable this 'gap' to feel filled. Again, provision should be provided in the form of guidance and counselling to help the individual adapt his aspirations to available and futuristic opportunities allowing him to adjust to a more realistic time-scale. This would enable the organisation to lower the risk of losing valuable employees and provide motivation and support to satisfy the individual and promote a sense of interest and worth from the organisation to the individual.

Career aspirations are also interdependent upon the wider economic environment. During periods of recession, when unemployment is rising, individuals tend to modify expectations down to a practical, workable level. Conversely, during economic expansion, individuals tend to adjust expectations upwards and strive for higher achievement levels.

In this section, manager development has been examined from an unconventional angle: through training and development (focusing upon how the organisation meets its own needs for skill and expertise), and from a career development perspective. Manager development could thus be seen as a dual responsibility. The individual and the organisation have responsibilities: the individual to contribute to the organisation and his career; the organisation to reward, develop and support and to ensure that its own needs for skills, expertise, appropriate management styles, and so on, are met. The next section looks at management development.

Management development

Management development is an ambiguous term. Finding a concise definition is difficult. Some see it as the development of a set of skilled tasks which when practised can ensure the smooth running of the organisation. Here the emphasis is on control and predictability, with individuals acquiring sophisticated techniques which can be translated and used to extract the maximum potential for the organisation. Leadership and management development are often confused and used interchangeably. Whilst leadership is an important component of management skill, it does not in itself embody management development completely.

Indeed, management development is all of these things. Managers need to develop specific skills. Organisations need control in order to operate effectively. Leadership is an important and integral part of managerial efficiency. Therefore, management development is the sum total of these component parts, but it is also the learning process which the individual undergoes. The objective of management development is to increase the competence of managers. The next question is how this can be successfully achieved.

Management development needs to be viewed with optimism. Too often it is viewed with a 'you win some, you lose some' attitude. Managers are thrown in at the deep end and left to struggle. Those who manage to survive become 'winners', those less fortunate are identified as 'losers'. But is this the best method? Incompetence should be viewed as the result of a set of problems which can be overcome through meaningful practice and adequate programmes providing managers with opportunities to build on strengths and overcome weaknesses through specific learning activities.

Management development needs good planning. A systematic approach needs to be adopted through which opportunities can be expanded for individual managers to exercise their skills. Training programmes need vision and imagination to encourage managers to commit themselves to the process.

Theoretical framework

Management development seeks to equip managers with the ability to adapt to ever-changing circumstances. To be effective it needs to provide opportunities to learn from experience and recognise that yesterday's solutions may no longer be adequate or appropriate to deal with today's problems. As Revans (1971) puts it: 'Those who would influence the world about them must, in turn, be influenced by the world'. A programme suitable for senior managers must consider the design of strategic objectives or corporate influences, the execution of these plans in the everyday world, and the development of managers as effective individuals under often stress-inducing circumstances.

Organisations have collections of tasks to be done, opportunities to be grasped and problems to be solved. A strategy needs to be implemented which enables the organisation to achieve its goals. Tactics need to be employed to meet the demands of the strategy. These include knowledge of technology and physical operations which are adequate to accomplish these goals. These can be embodied in the published procedures of the organisation or within the financial codes of the organisation. Revans (1971) gives the following example. The strategic plan may be expressed in the capital budget spread over several years. Tactical negotiations to carry out the plan may be processed through an array of operating budgets. The control of technical processes can be observed by a system of standard cost accounting. The implementation and control of strategy requires organising and cannot simply be limited to the person best qualified to deal with it; it must also refer to the factors which the system determines, of which he is a part. It then becomes a process of distributing information about tasks, opportunities and problems so that those involved can learn from the experience. The key to success lies in the fact that those involved can adapt and learn from experiences today how to anticipate and act better on their experience tomorrow. Personal and social learning are an essential by-product of the daily task and cannot be seen as separate entities but rather integrated and mutually compatible components of the whole. Managers need to develop the knowledge and capacity to make decisions, to negotiate effectively and to learn as individuals.

Revans describes three basic principles which influence managers based on the above. He refers to these as systems Alpha, Beta and Gamma. System Alpha refers to the use of information for designing objectives. Here the manager has to decide on a course of action, needs to anticipate probable outcomes, be aware of potential difficulties and find internal resources to deal with these difficulties. System Beta refers to the use of information to achieve objectives. This involves negotiation. Now the situation needs to be secured and its practical value assessed and tested through influencing others and seeing how it stands up to scrutiny. System Gamma refers to the use of information as a means of adapting to experience and change. The question becomes one of how the individual responds to the experience. Ideas have been tested and now need to be evaluated.

The manager needs to have an accurate awareness of the outcome in order to be able to learn from that experience. Any refusal to admit to faults or problems represents a departure from reality and any analysis of the situation in terms of a learning process will be barren; it is unlikely that the practical experience of the task can be used to enhance managerial effectiveness. If the manager is able to identify problems and discrepancies which have occurred and is able to change his perception accordingly, then he is learning.

Therefore, in order for management development to be a positive experience all three systems need to be first, identified; second, confirmed; and third, adopted with a strong degree of commitment.

Programme features

In-house training

This is a common feature in most management development programmes. Training is carried out internally, within the organisation. It may involve trainers employed by the organisation, or outside trainers bringing their expertise to the company, or a blend of these. The objectives of in-house training are to develop in-company skills and knowledge, and to promote an understanding of the organisational culture. Training ought to be tailored to 'here and now' situations to keep the organisation abreast of future needs. The structure of the programme should reflect the purposes of the organisation. One problem with in-house training is that it can remain static and fail to keep pace with changes in the organisation. Packaged training which is bought in by the company can lack applicability, and therefore relevance, to the organisation.

External training

This involves sending managers on outside courses. These courses can take various forms, such as academic degrees, short courses focusing on specific issues, clinics, seminars, or conferences. A principal spin-off benefit of such courses is that a wide range of managers from varying organisations and professions can gather together to exchange views and ideas, which is both stimulating and productive.

External training provides increased sensitivity to the outside environment that can affect the organisation. It also provides opportunities for personal development in an environment which is non-threatening, away from organisational rivalry and competition. This, too, generates a sense that the organisation's beliefs and values can be challenged in a way which is productive through interaction with others from other organisations. There are problems inherent in external training. A major problem is the cost factor. It usually involves not only a large financial outlay but also a large slice of the manager's time away from his place of work. It can also generate conflicts of belief between what the organisation stands for and what the manager learns, as he tries to apply it once he is back at work. It can also create more barriers between managers who attend courses and those who do not.

Job rotation

Job rotation can be used to increase the manager's sensitivity to the problems other managers have to deal with. It can also broaden experience and widen perspectives in a positive way. A spin-off of this can be to promote new ideas and skills which can be transferred to the manager's own specific role. However, job rotation does have disadvantages. It can have an unsettling effect upon managers and generate a threatening situation if not handled sensibly. It can also interfere with the smooth running of the organisation and unsettle subordinates.

Secondments

Secondment involves the usually temporary loaning out of managers to other systems. The main advantage to seconding managers is the cross-fertilisation of ideas which it generates. It can also act as a bridge-building exercise between organisations and, again, can have the effect of widening managers' perspectives. Problems surrounding secondment are mainly those of organisation culture. The problems caused by entry and re-entry can outweigh the advantages.

Mentoring

Mentoring is more widely used in the USA than in the UK and refers to senior managers assisting subordinates to grow into new jobs. Generally, mentoring is carried out on a one-to-one basis and its objective is to provide practical guidance to 'mentees'. It can assist in performance maintenance and also open up communication between the differing managerial levels. The problems with mentoring are that it can be viewed as favouritism and elicit jealousy from others; it can promote the dependency of the subordinate on the superior and thereby confine his growth. It is also an expensive and time-consuming practice.

Project groups

This practice sets up different departmental groups to work on organisational problems. It is viewed as a comprehensive way of developing managers as it has several benefits. Learning through cross-fertilisation of ideas enhances the speed and skill at which the group can work. It promotes an 'us' attitude rather than a 'them and us' attitude, which promotes a group sense and fosters good relationships between departments. Such groups encourage the development of task-orientated problem-solving abilities. Project groups need careful management in order to generate workable ideas and manage conflict between factions. Project groups ideally need experience in team-building to generate effectiveness and reduce disruption.

Case study: The consultants group

CAC Consultants is in the business of marketing highly sophisticated knowledge and professional skills, particularly in the field of project management. The key to the firm's success lies in the professionals and the skills they develop and deploy. Attracting and keeping first-rate professionals is a key issue, and senior partners hold strong opinions on it. The company comprises a chairman, six senior partners (each responsible for a major area of business activity) and 14 junior partners each reporting directly either to the chairman or a senior partner. In addition, some 40 professional staff and 60 support staff are employed, all organised into teams within the major areas of activity.

Some senior partners believed that career development is needed to attract outstanding young professionals. Another group had serious doubts about this, believing that the firm could attract people of the right level of skill. They also held that it was impossible to appoint more senior partners because of the impact this would have on the income of the present partners. Career development, they felt, would retain only the less able professionals; others would 'naturally move on'.

Both groups of senior partners recognised problems, however. For some the problem was how to attract and retain able young professionals. For others it was how to motivate effort and commitment from them in order to increase company income. The former saw the solution as lying in that of career development, the latter in the field of recruitment procedures. It was decided to hold a one-day meeting of senior partners to discuss the problem. Prior to the meeting there had been much discussion – with individuals often attributing various views or motives to others, who were seen as unfair, emotional, 'empire-building', overreacting or over-protective. At least one senior partner had been attributed as using career development as a means of rewarding one junior partner working for him.

At the meeting one senior partner proposed that regular reviews of individuals be carried out and that the senior partners should agree a policy regarding career development and promotion, both to junior- and senior-partners level. It was argued that this was not a panacea but would allow for modest improvement in present practice. It would not undermine existing practices, nor lead to a fall in the technical competence of the staff. Moreover, it was proposed that the process be largely informal and be designed so as not to threaten anyone. One response to these ideas was: 'I'm glad to hear that we intend to move slowly and build on present practices. The most important thing is to ensure that we recruit the right people and that they perform well.'

All agreed on the need to build up the firm's position. One pointed out that some of the junior partners were over-committing themselves in order to ensure promotion. Others felt that this would not matter 'if kept within reasonable limits'.

One partner passionately put the point that the firm's growth and reputation would be harmed unless they could develop new services to allow them to meet rapidly changing needs. It was essential to attract people to do this. Others responded: 'we don't seem to have any problems attracting people, and in any event we are highly profitable now. What's the problem?'

When the meeting convened several partners proposed that part of it be used to review the performance of the practice. Moreover, some partners' commitments meant that it had to end at noon, rather than go on to late afternoon. The performance review lasted until 11.20 a.m., allowing only a short discussion of the career development issue. There were constant interruptions as various partners were 'called to the telephone'. At the end the chairman summed up. Nothing would be done that was costly in terms of time and money. A subcommittee of the partners was to be formed to develop ideas and a policy. One senior partner asked that the subcommittee's representation should include the full range of views held. This was agreed. The meeting ended with much comment about the progress made.

A number of points emerged in interviews conducted after the meeting. First, the senior partners concerned to see career development progress felt they had to avoid anything which made other partners defensive. This would be seen as unreasonable. No mention would be made of the need to develop new ideas, services and businesses. Second, they also wished to avoid overstating their case because this would lead to the issue becoming personalised. Third, overall it was felt important to keep the discussion on 'rational lines'. Fourth, others clearly felt that the best approach to the meeting was to give those who wished to see career development 'their head'. 'Let them talk so they cannot accuse us of having our heads in the sand.' Finally, everyone appeared to rule out discussion of the validity of the views being put. 'If people are upset they become emotional and you cannot test their views.'

The case illustrates a number of themes from this chapter. We can see clear evidence of single-loop learning. Issues are not being explored. No examination has been made of whether or not more effective career development might lead to a means of achieving more effective business development (all agree on the need to build up the firm's position). Each 'group' of partners makes assumptions about other partners. No attempt is made to open up these assumptions. Thus defensive behaviour predominates.

Central to the case is the motivation of the partners, not the junior staff (although this is important). In partnerships promotion of staff will eventually lead to the appointment of new partners. Existing partners may see that as likely to create a dilution of their own equity in the partnership. Growth of the partnership can create greater rewards (for everyone) and allow the creation of more partners. But it involves risks. Do some of the partners really want to preserve their own equity? Thus, prior to career development the key need here is management development.

Moreover, we can see that the points on ineffectiveness discussed in Chapter 1 are also relevant. The partners wish to avoid defensive behaviour on the part of others. Thus they avoid discussion of the key issues. They do not wish to explore views for fear that emotions become apparent. The preference for the appearance of rationality is so great that open discussion is prohibited. Management development activities could usefully focus on this issue.

Concluding comment

This chapter has considered motivation, career development, and managerial management development. These have been examined together because in the world of management problems in any one area often involve problems in the other two. It has been observed that these problems link with how the organisation is structured as well as with the question of ineffectiveness. In the next chapter the structure of organisations is discussed.

Chapter 4

Organisation design

Introduction

It has been recognised for some time that the structure an organisation develops influences its performance. Such matters as the ability of senior managers to give effect to their decisions, the discretion available to middle managers, and the ability of management to motivate employees, are all affected by the way the structure is designed.

Most of us have experienced problems which may be a consequence of inadequate structures, at least in part. For example, if we order an item by mail and find on receipt that the incorrect size has been dispatched we will wish to return the item for a replacement. Suppose that a lengthy delay occurs in the supply of the correct item. This may well be due to commercial difficulties (the item may be out of stock) and/or inadequate communication between dispatch and sales departments. Were we to examine these problems we may well find an inadequate structure which causes employees to be unwilling to take responsibility for the complaint.

By organisation structure we mean the relationship between the different parts of the organisation. According to Porter, Lawler and Hackman (1975) organisations may be said to have the following characteristics:

1. They are composed of people and groups of people.
2. They are purposeful, goal-orientated social instruments.
3. They apply various means in order to accomplish objectives. There are two such means often seen as essential to goal achievement:
   (a) differentiation of functions and positions;
   (b) rational, planned attempts to co-ordinate and direct activities.
4. The activities and relationships within organisations may be conceived of as continuous through time and changing in so far

as organisations grow, decline and change, and people are promoted or dismissed, leave, or retire, and new people are appointed.

Traditionally organisations have been described as systems of formal authority, using an organisational chart, a simple example of which is given in Fig. 4.1. Many people argue that an organisation chart is misleading in that many important relationships of authority, communication or co-operation cannot be shown on such a chart. Many firms, indeed, avoid using them because of their controversial nature. Nevertheless, an organisation chart provides a means of showing a number of features:

1. The position of each management post in the organisation.
2. How the various positions are grouped into units (in our chart design, installation and quality are grouped into the engineering department).
3. How formal authority flows among them.

Formal authority is only one aspect of an organisation. In practice organisations function in far more complex ways. Behaviour within an organisation includes a considerable amount of activity outside the formal systems of authority and communication, often referred to as the 'informal organisation'. We define organisation structure as follows: 'The structure of relationships, procedures and arrangements which constitutes the organisation of an enterprise'. The relationships involved are those arising from the distribution of authority and influence and the allocation of duties within the enterprise. The procedures and arrangements refer to the means employed to organise and control work.

Bureaucracy

Probably the type of organisation most often referred to, bureaucracy may also be the most misunderstood concept within administrative practice. The literal meaning of bureaucracy is 'rule by the office' or 'rule by officials'. In popular usage it has come to take on a perjorative sense. It is necessary to distinguish between the bureaucratic model and bureaucracy as practised. As a form of organisation, bureaucracy allows enterprises to transcend the limits of direct control by the owners or by charismatic individuals. For the personal control of an enterprise to be effective it seems likely that three preconditions must be met:

1. The extent of vertical differentiation (number of hierarchical levels) must be small, thus allowing the direct communication of orders and direct face-to-face supervision.

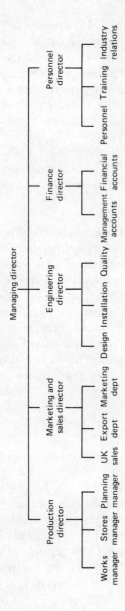

Fig. 4.1 A typical organisation chart.

2. The tasks to be performed must be carried out within a restricted geographical space, thus allowing the person in control to visit regularly the places where control needs to be exercised.
3. The range and diversity of the functions to be performed must be narrow; all members of the organisation must be involved in broadly similar types of work.

Clearly with the growth in size, range of products, degree of specialisation and geographical dispersion of enterprises, personal control becomes increasingly difficult, and professionalism becomes a core principle of administration. Organisations structured on bureaucratic lines are characterised by high levels of specialisation and differentiation between jobs and departments, by several layers of management, by standardisation of procedures and by formalisation (the extent to which rules and procedures are written down).

Bureaucracies can be categorised as either 'mechanistic' or 'professional'. Professional bureaucracies are common in public and private sector organisations. They rely on the skills, knowledge and expertise of highly trained people in order to function, and emphasise the power of expertise developed through long training. The mechanistic bureaucracy emphasises the power of rules and specific standards. The professional bureaucracy does not emphasise direct control by supervisors. Rather individuals are socialised into particular patterns of behaviour through long training. The mechanistic bureaucracy emphasises direct control and constant checking of performance by supervisors. The professional bureaucracy tends to be decentralised. Moreover, not only do professionals control their own work but they also seek collective control of the administrative decisions that affect them. It would be unusual for a hospital administrator to interfere in medical matters. However, the administrator would have more influence over decisions relating to budgets. Nevertheless, medical staff are likely to be closely involved in such decisions, commonly through meetings.

Most organisations which develop professional bureaucracies also require a wide range of simple, support or administrative tasks to be completed. The hospital requires cleaning, food preparation and records services, for example. In such circumstances there are likely to be parallel bureaucracies, one professional and decentralised, and one mechanistic and based upon direct control.

Matrix structures

Organisations dealing with complex projects need to ensure that the activities of different departments and different specialists are integrated. A line and staff, or functional, structure can be utilised. Thus, for example, accountants, engineers and computing specialists can offer advice from a staff department. A second approach is the project organisation structure; working parties, task forces or standing committees are appointed to deal with the problems of integration deriving from a project. Very often, however, there are strong arguments for maintaining both a functional and a project orientation. The matrix structure combines both these structures. Individuals are members of two groups, a specialist department (the functional department) and a cross-disciplinary team. Matrix structures can be relatively enduring or temporary, established only for the life of a particular project.

Functional and project organisations each have advantages and disadvantages, summarised in Table 4.1. The matrix structure attempts to overcome various difficulties by providing flexibility between projects and functional areas. The organisation establishes a dual authority structure. As a result, a matrix structure sacrifices the idea of unity of command. Whilst this can create difficulties, these are probably overstated. It seems likely that a matrix structure is

Table 4.1. Functional and project organisations assessed and compared.

FUNCTIONAL ORGANISATION

Advantages
1. Work is spread over many projects providing for stable manpower levels.
2. Interaction and exchange of ideas in the functional area are facilitated.
3. It is easier to concentrate on the development of the functional area within the company.
4. It is easier to justify large facilities such as laboratories, or marketing.

Disadvantages
1. Individuals may only be able to give part-time attention to any one project.
2. Responsibility for projects which cross disciplinary or functional boundaries is diffused.
3. There is a tendency to be functionally rather than project-orientated.
4. A project has no single focus point.

PROJECT ORGANISATION

Advantages
1. Projects have the full-time attention of individuals.
2. There is a single focal point for enquiries relating to the project, clearer responsibility and accountability.
3. It is relatively easy to cater for the requirements of the specific job.

Disadvantages
1. The experience of individuals is limited to project requirements.
2. There is little interaction within the functional area outside the project.
3. Leads to fluctuating manpower levels and skills mix on a particular project.

---

appropriate for organisations prepared to resolve internal conflicts through informal negotiation, rather than through recourse to formal authority. Thus a matrix structure may be appropriate for the organisation of skilled professionals, working within organisations dealing with large-scale and complex projects. A typical matrix structure is illustrated in Fig. 4.2, and the advantages and disadvantages of such a structure are listed in Table 4.2.

Having introduced some simple ideas about management structures we now turn to how these structures develop over time.

The development of the multi-divisional organisation

In the past 25 years business enterprise has undergone a remarkable transformation. From the early beginnings of small companies, managed by the founding entrepreneur, there have emerged large business enterprises which have outgrown their entrepreneurial family origins. Moreover, these large enterprises have needed to develop administrative structures and professional managerial competence in order to ensure continuity and to deal with the complexity of activities, possibly cover a range of tasks or products, and in which the enterprise might be involved around the world. For

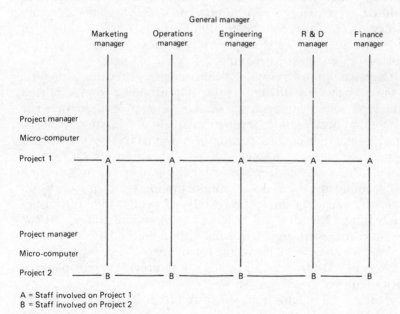

A = Staff involved on Project 1
B = Staff involved on Project 2

Fig. 4.2 A simplified matrix structure.

Table 4.2. Advantages and disadvantages of the matrix structure.

Advantages
1. Project objectives are now clear.
2. Co-ordination across functional lines may be achieved.
3. Resources may be used efficiently through negotiation between project and functional managers.
4. Teams of functional experts may be retained beyond the life of particular projects.
5. Information tends to flow easily between projects within a function.
6. A general management capacity can be developed through the project management post.

Disadvantages
1. Matrix structures are inherently more complex, making performance monitoring more difficult.
2. Priorities can be difficult to establish. Project managers will naturally consider their own projects to have the highest priority.
3. There is considerable potential for conflict between individuals.

---

example, a large construction company might be involved, nationally and internationally, in many kinds of projects, from road-building to the construction of power stations. For the business to succeed, a complex set of resources must be co-ordinated. Moreover, the activities of many subcontractors must also be co-ordinated and controlled. New patterns of administration have become necessary in order to enable the co-ordination, appraisal and planning of diverse and geographically dispersed activities.

Companies engaged in making a single product or providing a single service typically employ a functional organisation structure. The tasks of the enterprise are split into a number of specialised functions – sales, engineering, design, finance, and so on. The growth of an organisation, through expansion of existing markets, vertical integration or the opening of new markets by developing new products, creates problems of administration for such enterprises. The growth in size, in complexity and in the information flows required for the tasks of administration create pressures on the people managing the enterprise. In particular, individuals become 'swamped' with the detailed tasks of administration. At the same time, managers are increasingly hired on the basis of professional capacity. As firms grow, the members of the original owner/entrepreneur's family tend to be unable to provide the managerial capacity required by the enterprise.

The functional organisation structure brings a number of advantages. It is economical on management costs because it is a simple structure. Specialist and costly expertise is pooled in one department, allowing for the flexible use of such a scarce resource. Moreover, there are potential economies of scale (in engineering, for example, test and laboratory facilities). Members of a functional department will work with peers of the same occupational and professional backgrounds. Finally, clearer career paths for specialist employees can be provided within a functional structure. On this latter point, however, it must be observed that clarity is only one, albeit important, aspect of career.

When an enterprise adds a new product to its range (diversification) it will often need to hire people with the appropriate skills and experience. Commonly a new department will be established with a specific responsibility for the new product. Retaining responsibility for production, specification and quality with functional departments can create difficulties for the department responsible for the new product, partly because of the question of priorities and partly because existing procedures may be both inappropriate for the new product and difficult to change in the context of a functional department carrying major responsibilities for the existing product lines as well as responsibility for the new product. Such difficulties can lead to problems and conflicts between departments which begin to absorb the time of senior management.

The establishment of divisional structures has become the classical response to the problems of growth in size, complexity and geographical dispersion. Where these problems develop, the higher costs of duplicating facilities (such as design or engineering) in different divisions can be offset against the uncertainties, poor co-ordination and misuse of senior management's time which often develops in functional structures. In practice many companies adopt a mixed structure, retaining some aspects of functional organisation structure, perhaps within an overall divisional structure.

Alfred Chandler (1962) and Bruce Scott (1971) have advanced the concept that organisations develop through a series of distinct stages. This implies that a firm develops from a small owner-managed concern, first into a larger, functionally organised structure staffed by 'professional' managers, then into a large multi-divisional firm. Child (1984) has suggested a fourth stage in which the firm grows to the point where product and geographical diversification are so great that some form of decentralised matrix organisation structure (see Chapter 5) becomes necessary.

Case study: Development and problems of organisation structures

In this section we relate a part of the history of Courtaulds Ltd to illustrate the impact of the growth of a company on the problem of management control. The history of Courtaulds has been well documented and allows us to develop a number of points of general application. Coleman (1969, Vol 2) takes the story of Courtaulds from the beginning of the twentieth century to 1940. It opens with a discussion of the search for substitutes for artificial silk, particularly the development of international consortia providing for technical and other forms of co-operation, and the reorganisation of the company during the First World War.

After the war came the development of the rayon industry, within which Courtaulds came to occupy a major position. In 1921 the man who had guided the company as chairman (H. G. Tetley) died, and Samuel Courtauld IV succeeded him. During the next 20 years the company grew in size and diversity of operation, marketing and producing on an international scale. Furthermore, a firm which had been a textile business had become a part-chemical, part-textile business.

By 1928 the growth of the company had been such that it now employed some 20,000 people in Britain, had an American subsidiary operating five plants and had wholly-owned yarn plants in Canada and France, a share in a German factory and a large investment in the largest Italian rayon producer, as well as interests in Spain, Denmark and India. The problems of organisation associated with this growth in size and diversity were only slowly tackled. Coleman quotes a 1933 memorandum on internal management, drafted for the chairman:

The position today is that a company of world-wide activities is being administered according to a system which is really only suitable for an organisation considerably smaller and more limited in its interest. It seems as though this situation . . . has been on the whole deliberately perpetuated through a belief in the value of the 'man on the spot' having direct responsibility . . . Through fears of over-centralisation no adequate central organisation has been set up, and now matters of fundamental importance are decided by persons who naturally are unable to appreciate the full consequences of such decisions for the firm as a whole.

Five years later, in 1938, there was general agreement amongst some board members that organisation was weak and that 'the directors generally as well as the board were much too concerned with detailed administration'.

Over a period of years a new board committee structure evolved, with three main committees dealing with yarn, finance and textiles, and a series of subcommittees. Moreover, the company began to recruit a number of younger men from the universities to encourage new techniques such as costing and provide improved information and statistics.

By the late 1930s the company had a centralised structure, but the organisation structure remained unclear. Coleman (1969, Vol. 2, p. 237) notes that it was 'a long way from the multi-divisional decentralised structure pioneered by Du Pont in the USA'. The adoption of this type of structure was closely linked with product diversification and came later.

Channon (1973) takes the story beyond the end of the Second World War, when the company attempted to rebuild its rayon interests, at first unconcerned by the threat of new synthetic fibres. However, by the mid-1950s it became apparent that synthetic fibres were taking over markets formerly held by viscose. Diversification was sought through the acquisition of companies that manufactured paint, packaging plastics and underwear. Between 1962 and 1970 this acquisitions policy continued apace under Kearton. Now, at last, the multi-divisional form emerged. Kearton abolished the system of board committees which had previously linked the operating units and the board. Two were retained, dealing with policy and operations respectively. The operations of the company were divided into 70 divisions and subsidiary companies, each of which was a profit centre. Each operating unit prepared annual plans and budgets extending three years ahead, submitted to the operations committee for approval. Several functional departments at a central office department had supervisory responsibility, operating largely in an advisory capacity.

Over the years, then, increasing competition, product diversification, growth in size and complexity all led to decentralisation of operational responsibility, an increased emphasis on various managerial skills and the need for management development, and the development of a central office staff with an advisory/co-ordinating function.

The multi-divisional form: Problems and prospects

Diversification, because it may lead to divisionalisation, encourages the efficient allocation of capital and other resources within the firm, provides greater opportunity for management development, and spreads risks. From the perspective of the organisation, diversification followed by divisionalisation offers a number of distinct advantages. But once an organisation is diversified and then divisionalised, there may be reason to consider taking the further step of eliminating, or at least greatly reducing, its headquarters and allowing the divisions to function as independent organisations. The main problem on which this issue seems to turn is that of innovation. In essence the problem is that innovation does not thrive under central controls. Control systems used by divisionalised firms to minimise risk and co-ordinate efforts may militate against new ideas.

Moreover, any tendency for headquarters to concentrate on financial performance indicators (because of the size and product diversity, and because of a lack of time and relevant skills, this may be inevitable) may lead to a weakening of some aspects of overall control. The problem with performance measures such as profit, sales growth, return on investment, and the like, is that they can become an obsession, leading managers to become less concerned with less tangible indicators such as quality, customer satisfaction, and worker satisfaction with, and pride in, the product. It may be that attention to these 'intangibles' should be the core of top management attention in the organisation.

Finally, the growth of organisations brings with it the concentration of power into the hands of a few people. Galbraith (1977) develops the theme that giant corporations use their market power, coupled with their planning and marketing techniques, to subvert competition.

The multi-divisional organisation adopts a number of principles with which to manage growth and diversity:
1. Profit responsibility is allocated to the operating level.
2. Group or corporate staff are concerned mainly with planning and finance, and not distracted by the day-to-day problems of managing the business.
3. Profits are remitted to the centre which can take a corporate view of how best to allocate them.
4. Divisionalisation involves decentralisation and can act as a means of management development as operating managers take on increasing responsibilities.

However, Mintzberg (1983) has suggested that the divisional form may not be suitable in today's world. For Mintzberg the simple or entrepreneurial form is characterised by a strategic apex and an operating core (see Fig. 4.3). Communication is simple and work

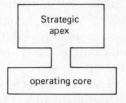

Fig. 4.3 The simple structure.

flexibly allocated. As the enterprise grows it must elaborate new structures. It cannot continue to rely on face-to-face communication. Thus specialist staff are employed. Support staff such as reception, legal staff and security staff are needed. In addition a technostructure is developed (Mintzberg's term) to provide services to operating managers; these might include work study, planning, quality control and personnel staff. Thus a division of a multi-divisional company might look like that illustrated in Fig. 4.4. In practice the danger is that a largely autonomous division might itself become as rigid as a functional organisation can become. Thus Mintzberg argues that multi-divisional organisations will only work well in stable environments. The main issue here is that the staff in the technostructure will focus upon achieving standardisation and control as a means of sustaining efficiency. This may well mitigate against creativity and innovation. One solution to this dilemma lies in the matrix structure (pp. 61–3).

Organisation design in practice

In practice the design of an organisation is subject to 'political' factors as different 'interest' groups come into conflict. The structures which do emerge often are a consequence of bargaining and compromise. But it would be unwise to see this in an overly rational way. The members of different interest groups are not totally 'rational' people, not fully aware of their own interests (which are still less completely identical with various groups) and do not have complete information about the present or the future. As will become evident when we discuss decision-making, this would be unrealistic in practice. Managers often take decisions on incomplete information, often 'muddle through', aided by the fortuitous nature of some events, and making considerable use of their intuition.

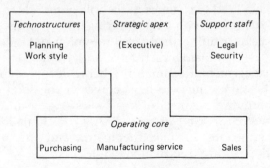

Fig. 4.4 A division of a multi-divisional organisation.

Moreover, the environment within which an organisation operates is neither fixed nor incapable of being influenced from within the organisation, through advertising, media campaigns, lobbying, research, and so on. In practice, therefore, there is a considerable amount of choice available to managers. Managers at all levels have discretion (see Chapter 2) and it is worth noting that this seems to apply to how organisations are structured.

In recent years there has been a resurgence of interest in general principles of management. These ideas have already been examined in Chapter 1. Peters and Waterman (1982) is perhaps the most widely known work in this area. Also the economic success of Japan has led many to examine Japanese management ideas. Ouchi (1981) has argued that the Japanese use superior models which could be imitated. Certainly ideas such as 'right-first-time' production quality circles and 'Kanban' production are worthy of examination (although not all are novel − 'right-first-time' seems little different from 'zero-defects', a quality programme initiated in the USA in the 1950s). However, as will become evident, these ideas demand new attitudes and changes to company cultures; this takes time.

New technology

Technological change as a major challenge to management today has already been discussed. The new micro-electronic technology is beginning to have a considerable effect on management. The impact of information technology and information systems is likely to be dramatic. For example, these developments allow increased management control both through the integration of systems, common databases and through the faster analysis of trends and results. Senior management can now obtain access to stocks, sales, credit control, purchase control and other data immediately.

Such changes may lead to changes in the role of middle management. Divisional structures with long reporting lines may disappear. The technology seems to aid further decentralisation and centralisation at the same time. In many organisations divisional staffs have been reduced, management accountability being devolved to business units. At the same time the new power of the information system allows more direct control of key issues (e.g. finance, performance) from the centre. Greater accessibility of information may aid the use of structures such as the matrix and the recently emerging 'federal' structure (see Handy 1984).

Control systems

Monitoring performance on a regular basis to form the basis of feedback and corrective action is an important part of the management task. It is related to motivation. Setting targets for performance is an example of using a system to motivate performance. However, there are many complexities involved. If targets are set for control, performance assessment and incentive payment reasons then staff may wish to lower them to allow a greater chance of success. If they are set as the basis of resource allocation then staff may wish to see higher targets.

In designing information systems we must take account of the purposes of the data. Moreover, data, being a source of power, can be used in damaging ways. Thus if the data demonstrate that a department is inefficient it should be published only when the responsible management team have had the time to resolve the problems. If data are used to 'punish', either directly or indirectly, then managers may well under- or mis-report.

Argyris (1964) deals with many of these issues in discussing budgets. Managers can become preoccupied with explaining deviations from budgets. Budgets can be and are manipulated by groups. If the manager of an operating department automatically inflates budget requests by 30 per cent to allow for the finance director's expected automatic reduction of those same budget requests then we have a 'game of budgetary control' (Hofstede 1968).

Most large organisations attempt to overcome these problems through setting budgets participatively and through extensive performance appraisal dealing both with performance and future plans for improvement. Many systems have been developed, a popular one being management by objectives (MBO). To set objectives for assessment purposes they must be:
(a) measurable;
(b) specified precisely;
(c) able to allow any factors influencing performance outside the control of the manager concerned to be taken into account;
(d) clearly communicated;
(e) realistic and achievable; and
(f) credible.
There are a number of dilemmas built into the use of such systems. Many argue that ideally the management of variances from targets should be under the control of the manager concerned. Moreover, performance appraisal, reward systems and budgetary systems should be kept separate. In practice this turns out to be difficult to

achieve. Nevertheless reasonably open systems, with effective participation, do seem to provide a reasonable basis for both control and motivation.

Organisation design, resources and complexity

From what we have said so far it is plain that organisation design is not a precise science. Yet there does seem to be evidence to suggest that issues such as control, resources and the complexity of the environment are important issues in organisation design. Lawrence and Dyer (1983) have examined these points in an interesting way. Their argument is that appropriate organisational designs are related to the complexity of the environment and the scarcity of resources for the organisation. Fig. 4.5 summarises this idea.

In effect Lawrence and Dyer (1983) identify what they feel are the most appropriate organisation forms for each combination of information complexity and resource scarcity (which might mean high levels of competition for sales or government restrictions on expenditure for a public sector organisation). Information complex-

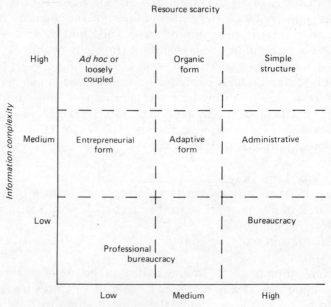

Source: Lawrence and Dyer (1983)

Fig. 4.5 Organisation design.

ity refers to the diversity of, uncertainty about and range of technologies and opportunities (and threats) in the organisation's environment. Fig. 4.6 reproduces Fig. 4.5 with typical functions substituted for each organisational form. For example, where markets are tight and the environment complex, the emphasis may well be on sales (to generate income) rather than on marketing (which costs money, takes time and may rapidly become outdated). This is a controversial view. Many marketing people will argue the contrary position yet the situation we describe is that of the trading company — which tends to do little formal marketing. In practice organisations attempt to control their environments to some degree. Is there a tendency to operate at medium levels? In any event perhaps most organisations find themselves operating in environments where adaptation and general management are both crucial. This is certainly the position taken in this book.

What specific changes are needed to move an organisation towards the adaptative structure? These are summarised in Fig. 4.7 (again following Lawrence and Dyer 1983), from which it is clear that these comprise either means of achieving more focus and business-orientated effort (or at least efforts more attuned to corporate objectives) or ways of developing people and groups to improve the emphasis on innovation. This seems to be instructive.

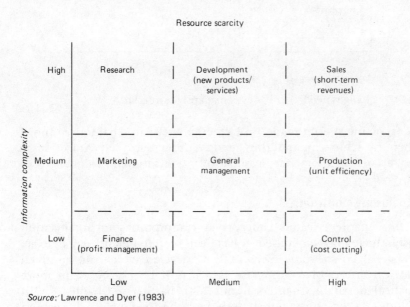

Source: Lawrence and Dyer (1983)

Fig. 4.6 Functional tendencies.

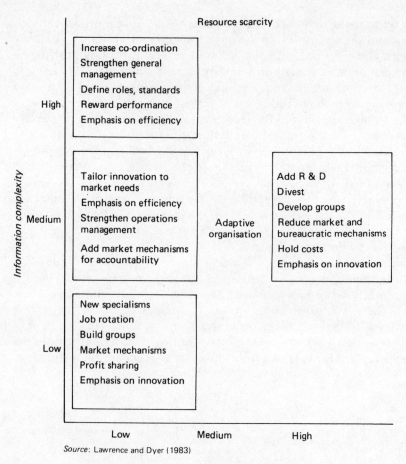

Source: Lawrence and Dyer (1983)

Fig. 4.7 Changes needed to achieve an adaptive structure.

Many of the points made will emerge again in Chapters 6 and 7 when the achievement of these ends will be discussed. At this stage they are left as a practical agenda for organisational design.

Concluding comment

In this chapter various concepts and approaches to organisation design have been examined. It has been seen to be far from an exact science. Even so, some ideas can be extracted which can be given practical effect. Many of these issues will be examined in more practical detail in Chapters 6 and 7. In particular Chapter 7 will include a case study which will be examined using these, and other, ideas.

Chapter 5

Developing corporate strategy

Introduction

To develop a corporate organisation it is necessary to be able to 'stand back' and take a 'broad view', to see the organisation as a whole. The ability to generate a 'vision of the future' is crucial. What is the nature of the organisation? What are the main strategic threats and oportunities? What major changes in the environment are likely to have an effect on the organisation in the next few years? These are some of the questions to which reasonably objective answers must be obtained.

The need for good strategic thinking in today's world is clear enough and has already been discussed. The pace of change in technology, market conditions and in political and cultural conditions presents real challenges. To acquire or discontinue activities, to enter or withdraw from markets, to restructure, redesign, automate production, to diversify or to concentrate on core businesses, these are all key decisions which will have an important effect on the economic well-being of the organisation.

This chapter will do no more than introduce and explain some of the key concepts and techniques of corporate strategy. The literature on this subject is vast and it is impossible to give more than an overview. Nevertheless it is hoped that the reader will gain enough to develop an understanding of how to go about this important work in practice.

Corporate objectives

What are the 'objectives' of the organisation? Obviously these may be stated in broad terms. Examples might be 'to increase the profit contribution of product A by the end of the financial year'; 'to improve customer service and quality'; or 'to improve the utilisation of resources'. Perhaps it is easier to distinguish these statements as 'aims' or 'missions' and then to define more precise objectives or targets.

Should objectives always be clear-cut and precise? Well, that such precision might not always be a good thing should have emerged from the 'administrators' case study in Chapter 1. Quinn (1977) provides four reasons to be cautious about announcing overly specific goals:

1. It can give people the impression that they cannot be changed even if reasonable arguments are put forward to justify a review. Thus creative ideas and initiative might be hindered.

2. It might provide a focus for opposition within the organisation. Organisations are political arenas, they are not simply places in which people work (see Chapter 6 for more detailed argument on this point). People who feel that they may be adversely affected may unite against the objectives, whether openly or not. The more specific the objectives, the more likely people are to see the implications.

3. Published goals are more difficult to change. General objectives allow flexibility as circumstances change. Given that the information available to those setting the objectives is incomplete, this would seem a pragmatic but wise approach.

4. Being too specific about objectives can risk providing competitors with valuable information, particularly if senior managers move.

This implies that the setting of objectives is a political process, particularly in large organisations. Certainly establishing general objectives helps in the processing of building consensus. Having general objectives overall does not preclude having more precise targets either generally or at the departmental or individual level. Crisis situations tend to create pressures for decisive action which can place a premium on more specific objectives. This point will be dealt with in more detail when the management of 'turnaround' situations is discussed in Chapter 8.

What kinds of objectives do managers pursue? Managers will often report objectives such as 'profitability', 'survival' and 'growth'. But in practice they may often seem to be behaving as if different priorities were important. For example, maintaining independence often seems a dominant senior management objective, particularly in an era of mergers and acquisitions. Whilst this may provide a spur to effectiveness, as many argue, it can absorb management time and lead to short-term priorities being overemphasised.

Strategic planning

Strategic planning may be defined as the process of identifying the different businesses or service areas within which the organisation is *and* should be operating, identifying critical factors for success, and finding methods of ensuring success. The focus throughout should be on action. A number of key ideas run through the strategic planning literature and there is much practical experience of strategic planning in organisations.

In an early and influential book, Ansoff (1965) described a growth model which captures quite a useful set of ideas in a simple matrix form (see Fig. 5.1). Similarly, the strategic planning literature seems to emphasise a number of very basic guidelines:
1. Leading from strength;
2. Concentrating resources in areas where the organisation has competitive advantage;
3. Concentrating on a narrow product/market scope at unit level;
4. Closing down activities if future earning power (discounted at the organisation's current cost of capital) is less than its liquidation value (not without difficulties, including computational ones, in practice).

Two of the most useful concepts introduced in the strategic planning literature of the 1960s were the learning curve and progress functions. The learning curve traces an individual's improving performance with repeated attempts at a task. The progress function traces a similar process. In essence the argument is that with high production volumes, costs fall for various reasons. Plotting unit cost against accumulative volume (for any product) on a logarithmic scale gives a straight-line relationship (see Fig. 5.2).

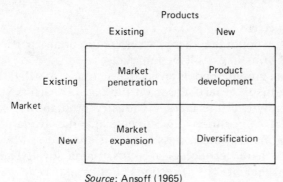

Source: Ansoff (1965)

Fig. 5.1 Growth strategies.

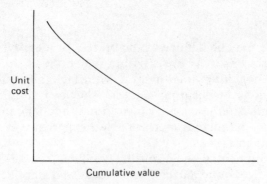

Fig. 5.2 The experience curve.

The experience curve is a function of the following:
1. *Product improvement*, including learning-curve effects, value engineering, methods and product improvement, materials improvements, planning and planned maintenance.
2. *Technological change*, process and product, improved materials handling.
3. *Economies of scale*, including financial and managerial economics.

Using the principle of the experience curve the Boston Consulting Group developed the portfolio analysis matrix (see Fig. 5.3). These ideas have been popularised by Hedley (1976; 1977).

Research in the USA identified factors important to profitability and return on investment, including the following:
1. Investment.
2. Productivity.
3. Market share.
4. Market growth.
5. Product quality.
6. Innovation.
7. The experience curve.

There seems little doubt that these factors are important, particularly for established firms in established markets.

More complex growth models are available (see MacMillan 1986). One defines industry attractiveness on the basis of factors such as the size and growth of the market, industry profitability, ease of entry, degree of competition, investment, and the availability of labour and raw materials. Business strengths are assessed by referring to market share, technological skills, brand loyalty and the quality of management. The Directional Policy Matrix (developed by the Shell Chemical Company – see Robinson, Hichens and Wade 1978) is shown in Fig. 5.4.

Market share

		High*	Low*
Market growth	High	Invest in market share	Segment market penetration
	Low	Acquire second largest company and fund market penetration	Withdraw

*Hedley (1976 suggests that whether a company's market share is described as high or low could be determined by comparison with the market share of its leading competitor, with a ratio of 1.5 : 1 being designated 'high'.

Fig. 5.3 The portfolio analysis matrix.

Industry attractiveness

		Unattractive	Uncertain	Attractive
Own competitive position	Weak	Disinvest	Phased withdrawal custodial	Double or quit
	Average	Phased withdrawal	Custodial growth	Try harder
	Strong	Cash generate	Growth leader	Leader

Fig. 5.4 Directional policy matix.

All of these techniques carry the danger of appearing too scientific. They are not and should not be allowed to dominate in strategy formulation. Note also that whilst portfolio analysis might point a management team in the direction of strengthening the cash base of a business it will not define new opportunities. These latter issues are more matters of process which will be examined in Chapter 6, where innovation is discussed, and Chapter 7, where creativity and the management of change are discussed.

The development of corporate planning

Before examining how the practice of corporate planning has developed in recent years, the basic steps in corporate planning must be identified. These are detailed in Fig. 5.5. In essence appraisal leads to the development of strategy through judgement, creativity and much else. From this can be established operational plans, annual plans, budgets and review. The most important point to re-emphasise here is that process is crucial. Systems do not create effective plans, people do! Yet without any system at all, effective plans could hardly be implemented.

Taylor (1986) has presented an interesting analysis of how planning has changed since the mid-1960s. First he identifies changes in the environment within which organisations operated. The period 1965–73 was a period of stability and growth. There was much emphasis on planning for new and complex (and often capital-intensive) technology. The phrase 'corporate social responsibility' was in vogue and participation was much talked about (if,

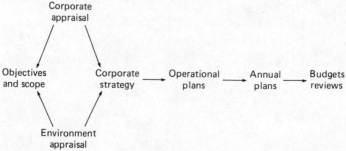

Fig. 5.5 Basic steps in corporate planning.

perhaps, not much practised). This also was the period when people pointed to the finite supplies of raw materials on our planet – the era of 'limits to growth'.

The period 1974–9 saw increased challenge to organisations in both the private and public sector. There was an 'energy crisis'. There was increasing concern about the environment. The quality of working life drew increased attention world-wide. Inflation grew apace.

The period 1980–4 saw decline, which caused unemployment, spending cuts and business failures. Job creation became an important item on government agendas. Competition with Japan was increasingly recognised as important. Turnaround management (see Chapter 8) was increasingly practised.

The mid-1980s have marked the onset of a period of revival, deregulation, increasingly global markets, emerging technological change, and a recognition that corporate cultures need changing if other changes are to be introduced. We are in an era of burgeoning information technology – but who will harness it? Public service organisations are under increasing attack as are large corporations in the private sector.

Taylor then examines how planning was carried out. The first period (1965–73) was the era of long-range planning. Long-term forecasts were made; five-year plans and budgets created. To do all of this various techniques were developed: technological forecasting, manpower planning, gap analyses, the product – market matrix, and budgeting, including programme budgeting. These emerged as inflexible, perhaps often leading to optimism (though this may perhaps have been a sign of the times). There was inadequate risk assessment, very little debate of fundamental issues and little or no assessment of social and political factors.

The second period (1974–9) saw the emergence of strategic planning. Increasingly corporate strategies were being made explicit (as opposed to a view of planning in practice which saw the next plan as an extrapolation of the previous one). Organisations were decentralised into business units. Increasingly senior managers created alternatives they called 'scenarios'. Now social and political planning became important. Techniques now included scenario planning, risk assessment, sensitivity analysis, zero-based budgets, and portfolio analyses. But often these processes appeared to be centralised and remote, involving elaborate analysis but not enough concern over the implementation of plans. Portfolio analysis tended also to undervalue the importance of linkages between products (for example, software, hardware and support services for computer manufacturers).

Thus the 1980s became the era of strategic management. Here the concern has been with both the development of and implementation of strategy. Business and corporate leadership are now important. The management of change has become a crucial issue. Techniques include competitive analysis. Values are increasingly analysed and debated. Integrated database technology has become the new 'utopia'. The new challenge is that of achieving changes to the corporate culture (see Chapter 1).

Competitive analysis

Porter (1980; 1985) has produced a soundly based analysis of competitive strategy and the means of achieving competitive advantage. The intensity of competition within any industry is determined by basic competitive forces. The strength of these forces, listed below, determines the long-run profit potential of the industry (measured in terms of long-run return on capital invested).

1. The threat of new entrants, which depends on the costs of entry into the industry and the likely reaction of existing industry firms. Important here are technological and capital-intensity issues.
2. The level of competition between existing firms and the reactions by others to moves by any particular firm.
3. Substitution, which presents an effective ceiling on price. Often a complex and difficult task, this involves the development of new processes.
4. The bargaining power of buyers, which is related to the intra-organisational model examined later (see Chapter 10). A buyer has power if it purchases a large proportion of a company's product or service, has the potential to integrate backwards (to produce the product or service itself), if alternative suppliers are available, or if the cost of changing supplier is low.
5. The bargaining power of suppliers, who affect an industry by their capacity to raise prices or reduce the quality of their goods and services. Suppliers are powerful if the supply-side industry is dominated by a few companies, but sells to many (e.g. oil industry), if substitutes are not readily available, if suppliers can integrate forwards (e.g. construction of oil refineries by oil producers), or if a purchaser buys only a small proportion of the supplier firm's goods and services.

To develop relevant intelligence on these forces a range of sources of data can be utilised, as listed below (Porter 1980).

1. Outside the company
   o Standard-setting organisations (for example, the British Standards Institute).
   o Unions.
   o The press, particularly editors of trade and local papers in areas where competitors' facilities or headquarters are located.
   o Local organisations (such as the Chamber of Commerce) where facilities or headquarters are located.
   o Control and local government.
   o International organisations (for example, OECD, United Nations).
   o Watchdog groups (such as the Consumers' Association).
   o The financial community (securities analysts).
   o Agencies involved in regulation, industry promotion, financing, and so on.
2. Sources of information about competitors inside the company
   o Market research staff.
   o Sales force.
   o Service organisations.
   o Former employees of competitors, observers, or service organisations.
   o Engineering staff.
   o Purchasing department – in contact with suppliers who call on competitors.
   o R&D department – generally follows technical developments and scientific conferences and publications.
3. Service organisations
   o Trade associations.
   o Investment banks.
   o Consultants.
   o Auditors.
   o Commercial banks.
   o Advertising agencies.

In a later book, Porter (1985) suggests that firms need to make greater use of scenarios to ensure that wider ranges of strategic options are considered. Moreover, this is more likely to create the circumstances within which assumptions are made explicit. He proposes the following way of developing industry scenarios:

1. Examine shifts in the major factcors influencing the industry (economic, socio-political, cultural, technological, legal).
2. Identify sources of uncertainty in the competitive forces (see above).
3. Identify the causes of this uncertainty.

4. Make assumptions about causation, for example, if looking at the motor-car industry make assumptions as to highest possible, lowest possible and most likely oil price.
5. Combine assumptions into internally consistent scenarios.
6. Analyse the industry situation which would result from each scenario.
7. Determine the sources of competitive advantage under each scenario.
8. Predict competitor behaviour under each scenario.

What, for example, would be the essential considerations in an examination of the world motor-car industry? The alternative strategies for car manufacturers might be the following.

1. The volume strategy: to match the volume strategy of the Japanese manufacturer; this involves raising levels of productivity, quality and reliability and cutting costs, sometimes by around 30–40 per cent.
2. Market segmentation: to become a specialist producer offering a high-value product (or a series of products) with unique features and services to a particular market segment – and so justify a premium price. This means raising productivity and quality performance as far as possible, given the low volumes available, and in addition the achievement of exceptional performance in those specific areas which are most important to the customers in the target market segment. The choice of a segment strategy inevitably raises the question whether the segment can be defended against attacks from volume producers with greater resources, lower unit costs, better distribution and service, and a larger customer base.
3. Diversification and internal expansion: to move out of traditional markets and proceed by internal growth or by acquisition:
(a) to become a component supplier;
(b) to assemble and/or distribute other manufacturers' products;
(c) to diversify into related products, for example from motor cars into trucks and tractors;
(d) to expand internationally.
4. Merger and rationalisation: to acquire or merge with other companies and then rationalise the various functions – R&D, purchasing and production, sales and distribution – in order to achieve greater financial strength, a stronger market position at home and abroad, economies of scale in production, access to new technology, management expertise, and so on.
5. Combinations and modifications: various combinations of these strategies are possible. For example, a company might adopt a

volume strategy in Western Europe and a market segment strategy in the USA; or a management team may decide on merger and rationalisation in their traditional markets in order to provide funds for diversification, and expansion abroad.

The corporate strategy will also need to be modified to match the prevailing conditions of world trade. In a fairly laissez-faire environment producers may continue to export from their home base. But if conditions become more protectionist they will be able to obtain access to national markets only if they manufacture or assemble their products locally.

Concluding comment

Plans are only of use if they are implemented. The discipline of corporate planning can contribute to manager development but planning will only contribute to the growth and/or development of the organisation if implementation follows. It is to the questions of implementation and change that we now turn.

Chapter 6

The conditions for effective change

Introduction

It will be evident that change is one of the key management tasks and responsibilities today. Whether in response to market, technological or social forces, the role of the manager is to ensure that changes are introduced effectively. To do so requires an understanding of three essential points.

First, change creates anxiety. Significant changes to an organisation are costly, time consuming and require energy and motivation on the part of those concerned. Only if people recognise the need for change, and can see the prospect of improvement, are they likely to feel the impetus to invest the energy and commitment needed. Change creates opportunities for the organisation as a whole, and for individual employees.

Second, change requires careful planning and implementation. People must be briefed, teams formed, resources made available, objectives set, progress reviewed, and so on. This demands careful programming. Only in this way can the problems which may arise, and any particular pressure points, be identified.

Finally, change and conflict are closely linked. No significant organisational change can be introduced without some conflict. Managers will hold different views about what needs to be done to improve an organisation. Determined and effective managers are likely to push their views forcibly. Thus there will always be organisational politics and conflict associated with change. It is important to understand and learn how to manage the politics of change in order that it turns out to be constructive.

Thus for effective organisational change to be possible there must exist the capacity to handle anxiety, to develop workable and acceptable plans and to manage conflict constructively. The next section examines three views of what comprises an effective or innovative organisation. It is argued that effective change requires effective organisation in the first place. In offering this argument, the commonly used distinction between efficiency and effectiveness is assumed, that is, that 'efficiency' measures the capacity to achieve the objectives set (in the terms of say cost, quality, resources, and so on); while 'effectiveness' includes not only efficiency but also adaptability, the effective organisation being able to achieve its objectives and adapt to changing circumstances in its environment. Argyris (1964) defines three core activities for any organisation: achieving objectives, maintaining the internal system, and adapting to the external environment. 'Achieving objectives' relates to the direct accomplishment of objectives – meeting delivery dates, quality standards, and so on. 'Maintaining the internal system' includes all the formal activities of authority and control, including training, budgets, communication and rewards. 'Adapting to the external environment' includes marketing, product development, public and community relations. Effective organisations will be those achieving an appropriate balance between the three core activities. The balance needed will clearly be influenced by the rate of change the organisation is experiencing, both internally and externally, but more of that later.

The innovative organisation

A number of management books dealing with innovation have been published in recent years. Peters and Waterman (1982) attracted particular attention. They identify eight characteristics of an innovative organisation, as follows:
1. Bias to action.
2. Proximity to the customer/client.
3. Autonomy.
4. Productivity through people.
5. 'Hands-on' management.
6. Concentration on strengths.
7. Simple structures.
8. Centralisation of core issues, and decentralisation of action/ implementation and day-to-day control.
In essence the emphasis is on getting things done, allowing autonomy as far as is possible to middle-level managers. Linked to this is a concern for individual accountability.

In much the same way it has been argued that 'excellent' or 'high-performing' companies emphasise the following:
1. Concern for the future.

2. A concern to develop human resources.
3. A focus on the product/service being provided.
4. An orientation to the technologies in use.
5. A concern for quality, excellence, service and competence.
6. An orientation to 'outsiders', clients, customers, the community, and shareholders.
7. Constant adaptation of reward systems and corporate values.
8. A focus on the basics of 'making and selling'.
9. Being open to new ideas.

Here the same concern for the basics of the organisation's business, whatever this may be, and the same concern to balance internal and external issues, are in evidence. For many organisations the concern expressed for the external environment, combined with quality, involves a new emphasis on service and on marketing as a means of achieving competitive advantage or more effective utilisation of resources and public support (notably, but not exclusively, for public sector organisations).

It is interesting to contrast these ideas with the view of what makes for an effective organisation which emerges from the organisational development (OD) literature (see Strauss 1976 for an excellent and critical review):

1. Lack of status differentials.
2. Innovation.
3. Sharing of responsibility.
4. Expression of feelings and needs.
5. Collaboration.
6. Open, constructive conflict.
7. Feedback.
8. Flexible leadership.
9. Involvement.
10. Trust.

This makes important additions to the first two sets of ideas. Open and constructive conflict is important as is the recognition of individual needs. Interestingly enough, the concerns are essentially, if not necessarily, internal concerns. The OD literature appears to give primacy to the staff and rarely mentions clients or customers. Nevertheless organisations which can create an 'organisational climate' which encourages those latter characteristics and achieves the balance of internal and external concerns referred to above seem likely to establish effectiveness.

Rickards (1985) has identified the key issues to be faced in deciding a strategy for innovation, as follows:

1. Innovation is systematic, and all the factors involved (social,

economic, political, technological, cultural, commercial) are interrelated.

2. Innovation is non-linear, it experiences stops and starts, and is often characterised by 'accidents' (for example penicillin).
3. Innovation is creative problem-solving, requiring imagination and flexibility. Managers need to learn how to support people, facilitate teamwork and problem-solving.
4. Innovation is situational, there is no one best way. Success will be dependent upon factors such as senior management support, sensitivity to market needs, effective communication and technological expertise.
5. Innovation requires appropriate structures; traditional hierarchies are too rigid. Project teams and task cultures are effective structures.
6. Innovation can be stimulated, but this requires major effort and involves significant learning.
7. Innovation requires various communities of interest, and customers and clients can and should play a part.
8. Innovation is mission-orientated, thus creating impetus, high visibility and a 'success'.
9. Innovation involves negotiation and participation; it involves conflict which must be resolved through negotiation or participation.
10. Innovation is itself innovation and will never go the way of past innovations.
11. Innovation and information are closely linked.
12. Innovation is personal and global; it involves and affects individuals and communities.

The same balance of internal and external concerns is evident here, too. But Rickards adds a number of ideas to the discussion. We can set out to stimulate innovation. Innovation is best encouraged in a task culture. Innovation should be mission-orientated. All of this suggests an active role for management in defining structures, tasks, project teams, in publicising success and in providing support.

In essence each of these contributions leads us to one central point. Innovation both is and requires organisational change. To launch a new product or service is itself to achieve an organisational change. But to create the conditions for this innovation it is necessary to achieve flexibility and organisational effectiveness. The conditions for effective organisational change must be established.

Case study: A financial institution

Company B is a large international institution with hundreds of branches in major towns and cities in its home country. In recent years it has been very successful, with growing profitability and turnover. Yet it faces major challenges, among them deregulation, new technology, competition and the growing complexity of the services it provides, both to private and corporate customers. The company is involved in a major programme of branch rationalisation. Some branches are being closed, others remodelled to provide either private or corporate services, others expanded as key branches. In the early stages of this programme of change it became clear that the company's property management department needed attention. Its performance was poor and its operations outmoded. Its capacity to plan and carry through the branch rationalisation programme seemed doubtful.

Property management was the responsibility of a central department employing 250 professional staff, mainly architects and surveyors, under a general manager. The general manager was drawn from the senior management team on a two-year posting. All general managers and departmental managers at that time had finance backgrounds. Indeed the culture of Company B powerfully sustained the belief that the only important work was finance. All other work, whether property, computing or marketing, was secondary. Career paths for non-finance people were limited. The extent to which non-finance staff were undervalued may be seen by noting that in the property management department no one could remember anyone having any training and development since the day of his appointment. The morale of the property management department was low and the level of inter-departmental conflict (between the surveyors and the architects) was very high.

The company was organised into 12 regions, each managed by a regional director. Property management at regional level was uncoordinated. Regional directors took many of the decisions without formally being properly accountable. Refurbishment decisions were under regional directors' control yet the costs of refurbishment were a charge on a head office account, not on the region's books. Moreover, the lack of co-operation between architects and surveyors diffused any professional input into property decisions taken at regional level.

Company B typifies the 'role culture' (the terms 'role culture', 'task culture' and 'power culture' are taken from Handy 1985) under significant external and internal pressures. Often stereotyped as bureaucracy, this culture is characterised by stability, prescription, rules and standards. Functional departments are clearly specified. This can be a very efficient culture in stable environments.

Role cultures emphasise high levels of commitment from individuals either to a department, or, in a professional role culture, to a particular profession. In this culture, position power is a predominant form of power. But in this case the stability of the 1960s and 1970s had been replaced by the turbulence of the 1980s. Now property management expertise was essential if the branch rationalisation programme was to proceed.

To detail the organisational change quickly, a property management professional was brought in to take charge and develop a modern property management strategy. This was only the second time in the history of Company B that a non-finance manager had been appointed at this level and the first time such an appointment had been made from outside. Under his control property management was decentralised to regional teams, managed by regional managers. Small teams, closer to the region, would be more likely to develop improved working relationships. Training and development were put in place for the professional staff. A career path was now opening up for them. All of this was moving property management toward a 'task culture'. Here influence is based on expertise, the expertise needed to carry out the task. Teams of people work together to achieve objectives and tasks. This culture places demands upon people but also provides for the merging of individual and organisational objectives. It is an adaptable culture in which the needs of the task predominate rather than systems and procedures. In this case architects and surveyors now work together more closely. Regional teams are managed by architects or surveyors. For professional purposes there is a professional development role played by a deputy general manager in the, now, small head office property management function. Arguably Company B has moved towards a culture more appropriate to the challenges it faces.

The organisational issues which must be faced if more adaptable organisational cultures are to be achieved are as follows:

1. Management autonomy, particularly with regard to reward systems. To what extent should local management have the ability to make decisions about gradings and salary dependent on market conditions and personal performance?
2. Interchangeability – movement across specialist or professional boundaries by internal promotions, fixed-term secondments, or short training periods – would help develop broader knowledge and experience. To what extent should promotion depend upon diversity of experience? Moves of this sort can sustain task forces or project teams. It can also reinforce individual autonomy, creativity and knowledge.

3. Openness or public testing of issues and problems would also be aided by interchangeability. People should be free to raise issues openly and seek solutions to problems, either directly or with the help of management.
4. Recent developments in management information systems seem likely to bring about systems which managers can interrogate. This will aid communication partly through the access so provided, partly by the promise of simplification of procedures and paperwork such developments promise.
5. Functional and professional advice can be provided to a more local level utilising task-team approaches such as that described briefly in the case study with professional development, planning and control being centrally organised. The focus should be on business needs rather than on professional demands.

Other organisational cultures have been identified. The 'power culture' is worth a moment's contemplation. It is frequently found in small, growing companies, including those concerned with property and finance. These organisations are highly dependent on one or more strong leaders. Control is exercised from the centre and decisions are made very largely on the outcome of a balance of influence rather than on rational grounds (which the uncertainties of our changing world will rarely allow in any event). An organisation with this culture can react well to change but the quality of top people is crucial. Individuals who are power-orientated, risk-taking and politically skilled will do well in this culture, where accountability is personal and direct.

One final thought on culture. The links between organisational culture, the tasks to be performed and the rate of environmental change have been discussed. But culture is of much broader significance than this. At home and abroad we often find ourselves working with people from different occupational, local and national cultures. Effective management thus demands the capacity to deal with cross-cultural issues and influences. The important skill here is that of 'empathy'. Managing change involves the need to influence people. Empathy, sensitivity to cultural differences, and the struggle to understand them and to communicate in an intelligible fashion, are essential.

The property management professional brought this skill to bear in his work with the professional staff involved in the change process described. Whilst these boundaries cannot easily be crossed, people respond to the attempt, and change programmes are all the more feasible and relevant for a leavening of cultural sensitivity. This skill will be discussed further in the section on coping with change in a later chapter.

The key issue of organisational culture emerges clearly. To achieve a more effective, professional yet adaptable property management department it is necessary to move toward a task culture. This demands openness, learning, good communication and the recognition of people's needs. Relating this to business needs is also important to give a clear sense of objectives and contribution.

Case study: Engines PLC

This manufacturer of engines, is a wholly-owned subsidiary of a USA-based multinational corporation. Its product is supplied to a small number of end-user companies. By 1980 the company was experiencing severe external and internal pressures (listed in Table 6.1).

This is a familiar pattern: a cycle of decline creating a major challenge for management to find ways of achieving improvement. The decline had gone far enough to mean that morale was low, resources scarce and management self-confidence was low. Thus the human and material resources vital in a period of change were not readily available. The most important thing to do was to develop an open attitude to change. The company had experienced little or no change in 30 years. Employees were accustomed to 'the way we have always done things around here'. Managers possessed little experience of, and therefore less skill in, the management of change.

Table 6.1. Internal and external pressures faced by Engines PLC.

External Pressures	Internal Pressures
1. Recession, high interest rates and falling orders	1. Inadequate organisational structures
2. High energy and material costs	2. Lack of confidence and fear of change, including the fear of redundancy
3. New products/materials technology being adopted in engine design and manufacture	3. Accustomed to slow change (or paralysis)
4. Increased competition both from abroad and because some end-users were beginning to switch to build their own engines	4. Limited managerial competence of managing change
5. Changes at group level as a consequence of a change in ownership	5. Lack of experience with new technology
	6. Low productivity and quality
	7. Ageing plant with attendant maintenance problems
	8. Low morale, high absenteeism, industrial disputes
	9. Cash-flow problems

New management at group level, recognising this company as in decline, brought in a new senior management team – a managing director, engineering director and finance director. The new team moved quickly. The strategy adopted is shown in Fig. 6.1.

The first step was to tackle the realities the company faced and to draw people into that process. Employees at all levels needed to understand the problems the company was experiencing. Beyond this it was essential that people be given the chance to seek out and develop solutions. Thus, on the one hand, openness in negotiations and communications with employees meant that the problems were better understood. On the other hand, through involvement of employees and by bringing in new skills (particularly marketing), new ways of doing things were sought. Employees were drawn into solving problems concerning quality, absenteeism, factory lay-out, and so on. Project groups from the design, a newly formed marketing department and the production departments became involved in seeking new products. People were given the opportunity to try out new ideas, to experiment, to seek solutions. This then started a process of attitude change. Recognising the problems and becoming involved in processes aimed at developing solutions led to a more open approach to the idea of change. Employees began to recognise the possibility that constructive, albeit not painless,

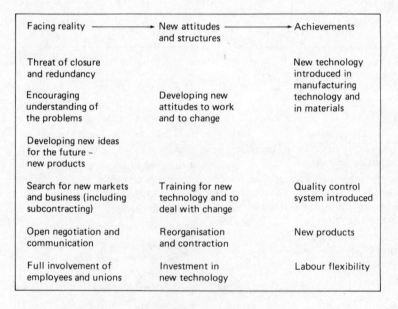

Fig. 6.1 Engines PLC: A strategy for change.

action was feasible. In these ways management and employees were facing the challenge posed.

Significant change involves learning. If problems and solutions are discussed more openly, if open or constructive attitudes to change prevail, then it is most likely that significant changes will be achieved. Change is possible without open discussion but only where people excluded from discussion and decision-making are not fully involved in the changes to be implemented. People not involved in discussion about changes can neither understand the need for change nor feel committed to the changes, let alone learn from them. One word of caution is needed here. Public or extensive discussion of problems in a declining situation merely creates anxiety unless a constructive attitude to change prevails, particularly within management. Thus to argue that effective communication will help without giving people the opportunity and support to seek solutions to problems will merely sustain the spiral of decline. In this company the discussion led to new attitudes which themselves both facilitated, and were in turn sustained by, training programmes for new technology, improved maintenance, quality control, the emergence of new investment and new equipment, and reorganisation (including the formation of a marketing department and the introduction of quality control systems). The spiral of decline was being reversed.

Most importantly, people started to understand the business more clearly. The problems of other departments could be recognised and considered. Managing change effectively involves *learning*, about which a number of observations can be made:

1. Learning is produced by exploring dilemmas (for example, improved quality was essential and end-users had to be convinced that they should continue to use the company product, but ageing plant, managerial problems and low morale made this difficult to achieve).
2. Learning is based upon personal experience and experimentation. People will only learn if they understand the problems and are brought into the process of seeking solutions.
3. Learning can be encouraged in a climate which encourages risk-taking, doing new things, trying out new ideas.
4. Learning requires the expression of deeply-held beliefs and will involve conflicts. Only then can ideas emerge and be properly assessed before being incorporated into new systems, products, strategies, and so on.
5. Learning can be helped by recognising the value of people and ideas, developing management styles which encourage individuals to contribute rather than to close off discussion and creativity.

Engines plc had by 1983 reduced staffing, improved the organisation structure, introduced a quality control system for the first time, achieved labour flexibility and developed new products. The leadership challenge faced successfully in this case was that of achieving change in the ways described whilst maintaining the business through very difficult times. 'Selling' the solutions to the group and 'buying' time were central to this and part of the politics of change, a matter examined below.

In Engines plc the following problems were evident:
1. Attitudes to risk were unrealistic.
2. The organisational structure was inadequate.
3. Strategies were too rigid.
4. Information was not available to decision-makers.
5. The calibre of managers was low.
6. There was a lack of innovation and change.

Again the case study illustrates a number of key points. Effective change required motivated managers and the necessary technological expertise. Most importantly it demanded that the company establish the conditions in which people would learn about the business, its problems, and about the expertise necessary to help solve these problems. Getting the right information to decision-makers was also important.

Diagnosing organisational problems

This chapter has discussed how to set the scene for effective change, including the issue of getting people to recognise the need for change by examining the organisation's effectiveness. One approach to examining the effectiveness of an organisation is to use an organisational diagnosis questionnaire. A shortened version of such a questionnaire is presented in Fig. 6.2.

Concluding comment

In this chapter, the conditions for innovation and change were examined and the diagnosis of organisation change was introduced. The organisational diagnosis questionnaire can be used in order better to understand strengths and weaknesses. These can be used in what is known as a 'force field analysis' (see Fig. 6.3).

If it is desired to achieve change it is necessary to move from the present state to the desired future state. Strengths can be exploited and built upon as part of the approach to the management of change, using the process of change to deal with weaknesses, using the

This questionnaire is designed to help you to determine the way your own company works, in a number of related areas. Assess how far you agree, or disagree, with the following statements as they apply to you within your own department, unit or business, using this seven-point scale, and circling the appropriate number.

1	2	3	4	5	6	7
Agree strongly	Agree	Agree slightly	Neutral	Disagree slightly	Disagree	Disagree strongly

In answering these statements, try to be as honest as you can. This is not a test, and there are no right or wrong answers. The only correct answer is what you decide yourself.

Statement	Answer
1. I understand the objectives of the company.	1 2 3 4 5 6 7
2. The organisation of work here is effective.	1 2 3 4 5 6 7
3. Managers will always listen to ideas.	1 2 3 4 5 6 7
4. We regularly achieve our objectives.	1 2 3 4 5 6 7
5. The salary I receive is commensurate with my performance	1 2 3 4 5 6 7
6. I have all the information and resources I need to do a good job.	1 2 3 4 5 6 7
7. The management style adopted by senior management is helpful and effective.	1 2 3 4 5 6 7
8. We constantly review our methods and introduce improvements.	1 2 3 4 5 6 7
9. I feel motivated by the work I do.	1 2 3 4 5 6 7
10. The way the work is organised produces general satisfaction.	1 2 3 4 5 6 7
11. We co-operate in order to get the work done.	1 2 3 4 5 6 7
12. Departments work well together to achieve good performance	1 2 3 4 5 6 7
13. People are able to cope with the pressures caused by change.	1 2 3 4 5 6 7
14. The work we do is always necessary and effective.	1 2 3 4 5 6 7
15. Performance is regularly reviewed against a set standard.	1 2 3 4 5 6 7
16. My relationships with other members of my work group are good.	1 2 3 4 5 6 7

Fig. 6.2 Organisational diagnosis questionnaire.

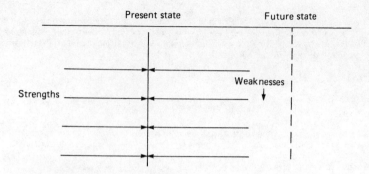

Fig. 6.3 Force field analysis.

learning which can be associated with change. In Engines plc weaknesses included the lack of experience of change, while strengths included the strong commitment of the workforce to the company. But note that to achieve change involved bringing in skills and ideas from outside in order to overcome the weaknesses. The weaknesses were overcome by demonstrating that improvement and change were possible and that management wanted everyone to be involved. The next chapter examines the managerial skills needed to manage changes such as those described in the two case studies presented in this chapter.

Chapter 7

Managerial skills for managing change

Introduction

This chapter draws together ideas on management skills, the management of change and the impact of organisation structures, systems and technologies on people. In Chapter 6 some of the skills for managing change were considered. Synthesising these ideas, it is proposed to outline the managerial skills needed for the effective management of change. First, planning change and the politics of change will be examined. Then a simple model will be used to describe how people experience major changes and how they can be helped to cope with significant organisational changes.

Planning change

Systematic models of the change process abound. But the issue in planning changes is about how to generate creative solutions to what are generally novel problems. Generally speaking, there is no shortage of ideas about how to reorganise, deal with problems, create new markets, and so on. What is usually missing is the framework and support appropriate to encouraging creative solutions to emerge. A range of 'blocks' to creative problem-solving are presented below as a means of looking at practical ways of organising and sustaining the process of planning change.

Blocks to problem-solving

As has already been observed, management support is a key to innovation. This section takes this a stage further to consider some of the blocks to problem-solving in order to enable a better understanding of how to manage this process. The ideas presented here come from Adams (1987).

Perpetual blocks

Stereotyping. We see what we expect to see. Over recent years there has been a growing awareness of stereotyping. For example, women only work for 'pin-money' , therefore there is no point in reviewing their jobs to see if they can be improved.

Difficulty in isolating the problem. A friend of the present authors gave a classic example of this recently. He was a member of a team of consultant designers given the brief of designing an apple-picking machine. All sorts of solutions were put forward. None seemed feasible – in general all were too big and too unwieldy. It was a month before a team member said "our problem is that we are focusing upon the wrong problem – we should look at the design of the tree". Eventually a new strain of apple trees only a few feet high was created. The problem of designing the machine then disappeared. The height and spread of apple trees had been the essential difficulty, not the design of apple-picking as such.

The tendency to delimit the problem area too closely. All too often problems are defined very narrowly. In the consultants group case study presented in Chapter 1, each group of partners defined the problem narrowly, thus neither faced the real problem – its own motivation.

Inability to see the problem from various viewpoints. The training and development of professionals (such as doctors, lawyers, accountants, or engineers) carries with it the risk that they will see problems only in terms of their own discipline; this is called 'trained incapacity'. Seeing problems from different viewpoints helps in conceptualising the problems. It also helps when support is solicited for solutions.

Saturation. Data may come in large quantities, and they may contain much that is relevant to the problem (see the case study on the Three Mile Island accident in Chapter 10 for an example).

Failure to use all sensory inputs. Though a great deal of data may be needed to solve a problem, there is a danger that not all the data available are utilised. For example, when trying to decide on a new organisation structure for a new venture the experience of other organisations in a similar position might be ignored.

Emotional blocks

Fear of taking a risk. The fear of making a mistake, to be seen to fail, is a common emotional block. If organisations 'punish' failure then this fear is at least realistic. Often, however, the consequences of a mistake are far from serious. Excessive importance is attached to the risk of failure.

Inability to tolerate ambiguity. The solution of a complex problem is a messy process. The data will be misleading, incomplete, full of opinions, values, and so on. Whilst creating solutions, plans, and the like, requires that order is eventually established, too early an attempt to do so may mean that promising ideas are missed.

Preference for judging rather than generating ideas. Judging ideas too early can lead to early rejection. The onus of proof is all too easily placed on the person with the idea. Yet if the idea is novel it may be poorly thought out and not present a good 'fit' to the hazy and incomplete data. Thus rejection is easy. Finding reasons to say 'no' is easier than finding reasons to say 'yes' – particularly for poor risk-takers intolerant of ambiguity!

Inability to incubate. This is an unwillingness to 'sleep on the problem' often because there seem to be pressures for solutions. In planning the process of managing change enough time should be allowed for ideas to incubate.

Cultural blocks

Taboos. These are issues which cannot be discussed and therefore cannot be faced. This was discussed in the administrators case study in Chapter 1.

Focus rather than fantasy. Adams forcefully makes the point that psychologists have concluded that children are more creative than adults. This might be explained by adults being more aware of practical constraints. However, he says, 'another explanation ... is that our culture trains mental playfulness, fantasy and reflectiveness out of people by placing more stress on the value of channelled mental activities'.

Problem-solving is a serious business. Linked to lack of creativity is the notion that humour has no place in problem-solving. And yet humour is often based on the process of associating apparently unrelated ideas. Creativity is the same, in that it often involves the association of unrelated ideas or structures. Adams argues therefore that humour is an essential ingredient for effective problem-solving.

Reasons and intuition. People often seem to believe that reason, logic, and numbers are good, and that feelings, intuition and pleasure are bad. Adams suggests that this is based on our Puritan heritage and our technology-based culture (which at least raises the question of how this point applies in cultures without a Puritan heritage). This has been complicated by the tendency to assign these characteristics to sex roles, namely that men are logical, physical, tough and pragmatic whilst women are sensitive, emotional and intuitive. Creativity demands a balance of these characteristics.

Tradition and change. Traditions are hard to overcome, particularly when people do not reflect on their traditions and their present problems/dilemmas together. We need tradition − it is on our traditions that much of our personal commitment and motivation is based. We need respect for tradition and to recognise the need for change.

Adams distinguishes primary and secondary creativity. Primary creativity generates the structures and concepts which allow the solution of a family of problems. Secondary creativity deploys these structures and concepts to develop and improve particular solutions. He argues that primary creativity demands more intuition, humour, feeling and emotion. Secondary creativity seems more likely to be associated with logic and reason − as the structures already established are deployed systematically to solve specific problems within a now well-understood field. Secondary creativity involves applying rules − primary creativity requires that existing rules be ignored, so that new rules can be generated (precisely what Sir Isaac Newton did!).

Environmental blocks

Lack of support. It has already been observed that a non-supportive environment is not conducive to innovation − or creative problem-solving. Change is often seen as threatening and new ideas are easily stopped, by ignoring them, by laughing at them, by over-analysing them too early.

Not accepting and incorporating criticism. Those with good ideas can create blocks, by not being willing to accept criticism. Doing so builds an atmosphere of trust and support, and leads to improvements in what will necessarily have been an imperfect idea.

Bosses who know the answer. Many a manager is successful because he has ideas and can push them through. But only if such a manager will listen to subordinates will he be able to utilise his creativity.

Cognitive blocks

Using the incorrect language. Whether mathematical, professional (e.g. accounting or marketing, or visual, using an inappropriate language can hinder creativity in problem-solving. The language and concepts of accounting tend to emphasise short-term and quantitative criteria, which can create blocks to creativity if the creative idea is ambiguous and, as yet, ill-formed.

Inflexible use of strategies. There are many strategies available; they are often used unconsciously but not necessarily to best effect in problem-solving, perhaps because of the various blocks already discussed.

Lack of the correct information. This is clearly a limiting factor. But again balance is needed. Information makes him who has it an expert. But if he thinks down the lines of that expertise – he can run the risk of being closed off from creative solutions.

Working through the blocks

This is what Adams calls 'block-busting'. Various techniques are available. Here it is not necessary to do more than list one or two very briefly. More detail can be found by referring to Adams's own account. Identifying the blocks in the first place helps enormously! A questioning attitude will help. Various thinking aids can also be applied, including attribute-listing, 'checklists' and list-making. Being able to suspend judgement as an individual or in a group can enhance creativity. Another useful technique is 'synetics' (Gordon 1961).

These following actions or attitudes seem to encourage creativity in problem-solving:
1. Staying loose or fluid in one's thinking until rigour is needed.
2. Protecting new ideas from criticism.
3. Acknowledging good ideas, listening, showing approval.
4. Eliminating status or rank.
5. Being optimistic.

  6. Supporting confusion and uncertainty.
  7. Valuing learning from mistakes.
  8. Focusing on the good aspects of an idea.
  9. Sharing the risks.
10. Suspending disbelief.
11. Building on ideas.
12. Not evaluating too early.

The following actions or attitudes seem to discourage creativity:

  1. Interrupting, criticising.
  2. Being competitive.
  3. Mocking people.
  4. Being dominant.
  5. Disagreeing; arguing; challenging.
  6. Being pessimistic.
  7. Pointing out flaws.
  8. Being inattentive, not listening, using silence against people.
  9. Reacting negatively.
10. Insisting on 'the facts'.
11. Giving no feedback, acting in a non-committal manner.
12. Pulling rank.
13. Becoming angry.
14. Being distant.

Limits on problem-solving

Still more limits or 'blocks' can be listed. At the individual level people may engage in 'satisficing' or 'incrementalism', accepting satisfactory solutions and or/making only incremental or limited changes to previous policies.

At the group level there are 'group think' and 'risky shift'. 'Group think' is characterised by complacency and lack of critical evaluation of ideas. 'Risky shift' is a condition observed in experimental groups where groups seem likely to take more risk decisions than the individuals involved might have opted for (diffusion of responsibility perhaps) but still without critical examination. At the organisational level various typical limits can be identified. Some have already been observed. People seem to 'distance' themselves from problems. Where organisations are highly centralised responsible managers may be 'out of touch'. There can exist an 'illusion of reliability' in existing techniques or people (the Greeks had a word for this – 'hubris' – which means overbearing arrogance). Highly specialised organisations can lead to parochialism, the tendency to conceal dissent or disagreement, and to problems of communication see Chapter 4). Solutions to all of these limits involve opening up the problem-solving process, being willing to change and allowing the 'block-busters' to operate. The assumption is that the ideas are there, amongst the people – the challenge is to encourage them, to help them find expression, then to evaluate realistically, to apply and learn and then to change. This can be summarised in Fig 7.1.

Dealing with organisational politics

So far so good! But organisations are 'political'. Individuals and groups pursue varying and often different interests. Many people will not be (or feel) so involved in the planning process that they accept full commitment to implementation. Conflict is a necessary part of change, so it is important to learn to deal with the politics of change.

To manage change we need to understand and handle corporate politics. Often ignored or disguised under terms such as 'effective communications', if managers are to encourage action and achieve change they need to work within the corporate politics. They must understand political power bases and how to use them. Political power bases include expertise, personal credibility, and formal or perceived status. More durable power bases may be control over information, access to influential senior managers and group support. In thinking about the management of change we must focus on the tactics of employment. Perhaps most important are the following:

1. Understanding and using networks. Identify the key managers and other staff who can have an influence on the change. Time spent discussing ideas and clearing proposals with them is time well spent. Reference to the power bases of all the people involved will identify what networks exist.

| | | Problem solving | |
		Restricted (to top management team)	Extended
Attitude to change	Negative	Little learning or change feasible	Anxiety likely to be created
	Positive	Learning & change can occur *but* only if there is no significant opposition likely from those who have not been involved	Learning and change possible

Fig. 7.1 Learning from change.

2. Managing the information politically. Sometimes controversial schemes can be put into effect if included as a small part of some other project. Sometimes schemes can be put through piecemeal. A study might be set up to generate the 'data' – evidence is thus created which cannot be easily ignored.

Managers, and others, utilise a variety of resources as they engage in the politics of organisation. They may have *formal authority*, or may be perceived as having such, by virtue of their position. Moreover, they may have *direct control over resources*. The use of a resource control to negate change programmes is widely practised. If a change programme needs engineering resources, and if the engineering manager can withhold those resources, perhaps by claiming that other priorities must prevail, then change can be delayed. Control of information, agenda and access are all important political resources. It is commonplace to say 'information is power': the power to control the organisation internally, the power to influence the development of future policy. This point was made by Henry Kissinger (1979) when he discussed the new role President Nixon and he had agreed for the National Security Council at the beginning of Nixon's first term.

A president should not leave the presentation of his options to one of the Cabinet departments or agencies. Since the views of the departments are often in conflict, to place one in charge of presenting the options will be perceived by the others as giving it an unfair advantage. Moreover, the strong inclination of all departments is to narrow the scope for Presidential decision, not to expand it. They are organised to develop a preferred policy, not a range of choices. If forced to present options, the typical department will present two absurd alternatives as straw men bracketing its preferred option – which usually appears in the middle position. A totally ignorant decision-maker could easily satisfy his departments by blindly choosing Option 2 of any three choices which they submit to him. Every department, finally, dreads being overruled by the President: all have, therefore, a high incentive to obscure their differences. Options tend to disappear in an empty consensus that at the end of the day permits each agency or department maximum latitude to pursue its original preference. It takes a strong, dedicated and fair Presidential staff to ensure that the President has before him genuine and not bogus choices.

Recognising the narrowness of view which often emerges from specialist, departmental and sometimes from professional concerns, Kissinger here demonstrates the crucial importance of controlling the presentation of options to a president. Without doing so the president may be at the mercy of departments. Departments may preclude policy debate by the nature and range of the options presented to the president. They may also structure a policy debate by purposely obscuring differences over policy in the pursuit of consensus.

Processes and forms of politics

The forms the politics of organisational change may take are varied. Fairly obviously, budgets, career development, succession planning systems, structures, appraisal and reward systems have political dimensions. Decisions in such areas will carry a political element. We might say that this is undesirable but we should not close our minds to the possibility that the reality is different from what some would say is the ideal. To understand decisions within a budgeting context, we must consider political issues. In much the same way, to understand how changes are implemented, we need to recognise the resources, processes and forms of politics.

In facing the complexity of organisations, including the complexity created by the politics of change, a few simple 'rules of thumb' seem worth considering (without suggesting that they serve as an infallible guide to action!).

1. There are some things little can be done about in practice:
   (a) decision-making is neither rational nor orderly (indeed we have seen that it is perhaps as well that this is so if we seek creative solutions);
   (b) conflicting demands for resources, priorities, attention;
   (c) uncertainty;
   (d) external or environmental forces.
2. There seem to be some things top managers can do to support creative solutions and adaptable organisations:
   (a) set appropriate values;
   (b) support problem-solving and risk-taking;
   (c) design systems (e.g. reward systems) to support action;
   (d) focus on the manageable;
   (e) develop skills in people.
3. There seem to be some things top managers can do to support the implementation of change:
   (a) devote time to implementation activities and issues;
   (b) interpret history and traditions around the solutions (by reference to the actions of key people in the history of the business, organisation or industry);
   (c) use simple phrases in support of change ('quality is the key'; 'right first time'; 'pursuit of excellence').
4. There are some things middle managers seem able to do:
   (a) choose the problems to work on, the battles to fight and when to compromise;

(b) develop an excellent knowledge of the organisation and its people;

(c) develop their own skills.

No guarantees here, mere pragmatism. This is perhaps not perfect, though it has been said that 'the perfect is the enemy of the good'.

Coping with major organisational changes

Thus far some of the managerial skills associated with the effective management of change have been considered. This section will consider the impact of change upon the people directly affected, which will often include many middle and senior managers. The concern here is with the people who must take on new tasks, develop new skills, be transferred, regraded or retrained. Once changes emerge people must learn to cope as individuals. A simple model will be used to describe how people experience change and then consider how they can cope with the pressures created by change. Understanding this can allow senior managers to provide practical support for people undergoing change and may better enable them to avoid creating constraints on people which make their personal task of coping all the harder.

Often the problems of implementing change are discussed as 'resistance to change'. In fact the change situation is both more complex than this phrase suggests and capable of a more constructive interpretation. Managers often encourage 'resistance to change' by dealing with people as if that is the response they expect. Here the practical and positive steps which can be taken to support people as they cope with change are considered.

Change creates uncertainty, anxiety and stress. Moreover, changes which have a big impact on the work people do will affect their self-esteem. So much is well established (see Cooper 1981; Miller and de Vries 1985; Kirkpatrick 1985). Linked to this impact on self-esteem will be a performance effect. In fact in periods of change performance is affected in three ways:

1. The new systems, processes, methods, and so on, have to be learned. This takes time and there is a *learning curve effect*.
2. There is a *progress effect*. As the new system is installed and commissioned, snags are ironed out and modifications introduced to achieve performance improvement. New systems do not work perfectly from the outset.
3. Finally, there is the *effect of self-esteem*. Significant organisational changes create a decline in self-esteem for many of those directly affected. This will effect performance. Whilst the links of satisfac-

tion and self-esteem with performance are complex and not fully understood there seems to be some association of these factors. The links between these ideas and 'the experience curve' discussed in Chapter 5 should be noted.

In practice performance will decline once major changes are under way as a result of a combination of these factors. The view of the present authors is that the main driving force to rebuilding performance quickly will be rebuilding self-esteem. This can be helped by action of the learning curve and progress fronts. The model consists of five stages. These are capable of more detailed analysis but for the present purposes this simplified form seems workable. The model (see Fig.7.2) is drawn, in particular, from the work of Adams, Haynes and Hopson (1976) on coping with personal life changes.

Stage 1: Denial

'We have always done things this way!' 'Why change, we are making a profit, aren't we?' 'Don't change a winning team.' These are some of the ways denial can find expression. Faced with the possibility of change people will often find value in their present circumstances; often in work situations which they have complained of previously. This apparent paradox should not be surprising. People are impelled by contradictory motivations. Coal miners

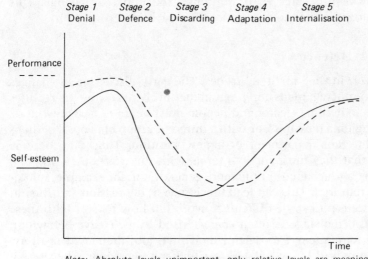

Note: Absolute levels unimportant, only relative levels are meaningful. Problems of measurement are significant but do not obscure the assessment of relative levels of performance or self-esteem.

Fig. 7.2 The coping cycle.

threatened with the closure of a pit will defend their pit and jobs with some vigour, yet still believe fervently that working conditions are arduous and even dangerous.

If major organisational changes come suddenly and dramatically then a kind of paralysis can often occur. People seem overwhelmed, unable to plan or even understand what is going on. Often there is a longish period of gestation as ideas are discussed and concrete changes planned. If these changes are not particularly new or dramatic then this paralysis may be felt just as intensely. However, the tendency to deny new ideas, at least at first, does seem to be a fairly general reaction. The advantages of the present situation are emphasised and attachments to the job, the work-group and the existing skills are recognised.

Thus it is that self-esteem can increase, particularly if the presence of an external threat leads to increased group cohesion. If self-esteem does increase performance is unlikely to improve, either because the discussion of impending change can absorb energy, or because often there are systems in place which may hold back performance improvement – for example, payment systems. If the change is dramatic, novel and traumatic, involving, say, a sudden job change or redundancy, then this stage can involve an immediate decline in performance. Generally, however, there is a warning period and performance will not decline immediately. One way individuals respond at this stage is to 'minimise' the impact of change. This allows people time to face up to a few realities.

Stage 2: Defence

However, in time reality obtrudes. The early discussion of changes leads to concrete plans and programmes of change. Now the realities of change become clearer and people must begin to face new tasks, working for a new boss, or with a different group of people, perhaps in a different department or a new location. Thus they become aware that they must come to terms with the way they work, and perhaps with changes in life more generally, if, for example, relocation is required. This can lead to feelings of depression and frustration because it can be difficult to work out how to deal with these changes. This stage is often characterised by defensive behaviour. People may attempt to defend their own job, their own territory. Often this will be articulated as ritualistic behaviour. The present authors can remember the introduction of computer-aided learning in business schools many years ago. Many embraced these developments enthusiastically. Many simply rejected them: 'my subject is unsuitable'. One colleague provided an impressive show of activity on the computer, finally concluding that after much effort he had failed to make computer-aided learning work for that subject. Years later computer-aided learning in that subject is commonplace. Was this a ritual? Again this defensive behaviour seems to have the effect of creating time and 'space' to allow people to come to terms with the changes.

Stage 3: Discarding

There now emerges a process of discarding. The previous stages have focused powerfully upon the past. Now people begin to let go of the past and look forward to the future. We do not know how this happens. We know that support can be helpful, as can providing people with the opportunity to experiment with new systems without the pressure of formal training programmes, and so on. Now it is possible for optimistic feelings to emerge. It may well be that the discarding process is impelled by an awakening sense that the present anxieties are just too much to bear, or that perhaps the future is not as forbidding as it first seemed. Now behaviour may be observed which appears to identify the individual with the changes involved. He will start to talk openly and constructively about the new system. He will ask questions about it. In a sense he will say 'Well, here it is – we are committed to it – here's how I see it'. People may begin to solve problems, take the initiative and even demonstrate some leadership. Thus it is that self-esteem improves.

Discarding is initially a process of perception. People come to see that the change is both inevitable and/or necessary. It becomes apparent to them. Adaptation starts with recognition. Here we see human courage in difficult circumstances as the individual accepts new 'realities'. This can be exciting for individuals and groups. Taking the risks of publicly facing a new reality there is a sense in which they re-establish their own identity; the identity which may have seemed threatened by the changes being introduced. Thus it is that self-esteem begins to flow back like the returning tide.

The crisis of change creates great tensions within those involved. This creates many reasons for people to feel upset and disorientated. A new job appears to be of lesser status than the old one, valued skills seem unnecessary, the new work appears to be frustrating. The new system appears to be unusual, even frightening, although with practice it becomes commonplace. The crucial point is that this process needs time. Discarding involves experimenting and risk. Time is needed for individuals to re-create their own sense of identity and self-esteem as they 'grow' into the new situation.

Stage 4: Adaptation

Now a process of mutual adaptation emerges. Rarely do new systems, procedures, structures or machines work effectively first time. Individuals begin to test the new situation and themselves, trying out new behaviours, working to different standards, working out ways of coping with the changes. Thus the individual learns. Other individuals also adapt. Fellow workers, supervisors and managers all learn as the new system is tried out. Finally, technical and operational problems are identified and modifications made to deal with them; thus progress is made.

Significant amounts of energy are involved here. Often the process of trial and error, of effort and setback, and the slow building of performance can be a source of real frustration. In these circumstances people can evince anger. This is not resistance to change. Rather it is the natural consequence of trying to make a new system work, experiencing partial or complete failure, which may or may not be under the control of the individuals concerned. This anger is not evidence of attempts to oppose but rather articulates the feelings of those trying to make the new system work. Whilst managers should ensure the right training and support is available, they should generally remain in the background, allowing the people directly involved to make it work. By doing so these people will develop the skills, understanding and attachments needed for the system to be run effectively in the longer term.

Stage 5: Internalisation

Now the people involved have created a new system, process and organisation. New relationships between people and processes have been tried, modified and accepted. These now become incorporated into understandings of the new work situation. This is a cognitive process through which people make sense of what has happened. Now the new behaviour becomes part of 'normal' behaviour.

It seems that people experience change in these ways, initially as disturbance, perhaps even as a shock, then coming to accept its reality, testing it out and engaging in a process of mutual adaptation and, finally, coming to terms with it. Self-esteem and performance vary, initially declining, and then growing again. The variation of performance flows from mutually reinforcing individual and operational causes, as has been observed. The 'engine' for rebuilding performance is the self-esteem of the people involved.

It is not suggested that people go through these stages neatly, not that all go through them at the same time, or at the same rate. Some may not go beyond the denial of change. The important point is that people do seem to experience significant changes in these ways and this leads on to a number of practical ways in which the problems of coping can be handled.

Coping with the process of change places demands on the individuals involved. Various issues need to be faced either by the individuals or by managers. Note, however, that these issues are of concern to all affected by an organisational change, including managers.

Rebuilding self-esteem

The ground covered in this section is summarised in Fig.7.3. Simplifying somewhat, it is suggested that individuals have four main categories of need if they are to rebuild their self-esteem during a programme of organisational change. They need intelligible information. They will probably need to develop new skills, even if only the skills of dealing with new people as colleagues or supervisors. They will need support to help them deal with the problems. Encouragement to try out new systems is important. Provision of short workshops planned to achieve part or all of the work discussed in the preceding section can help. Technical support to solve problems is often needed. Access to people who can help is useful. Control over the rate of personal learning should be possible. All of these things can help, but most of all they need to

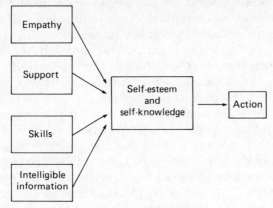

Fig. 7.3 Rebuilding self-esteem.

be treated with empathy. First and foremost empathy, understanding, is a key issue. The skill of empathy is the struggle to understand. People can never fully see a situation as others see it. But they can struggle to try and individuals will respond to that struggle. They will also respond to someone who clearly does not try. Making information intelligible to its recipient requires this skill. People need to try to see things as the recipient will in order to communicate. Often people do not try. If they pass on the information they have, they usually do so without attempting to make it intelligible.

Concluding comment

This section has discussed ways and means of introducing major changes effectively. Here one crucial point must be stressed. Effective organisations are those which introduce change quickly and in which people, employees and managers, learn about the business as this process proceeds. Achieving change without learning is possible, but sometimes not without a struggle, if powerful groups are opposed. Introducing change in ways which do not encourage learning is likely to entrench negative attitudes to change in the future. Only if people and organisations change, by learning from the experience of change, can effectiveness be achieved and sustained. A range of ideas and practical steps have been gathered to help people manage change effectively.

All these ideas and steps need to be integrated for effectiveness. Only if transitions are managed effectively can learning and change occur. This also acts as a constructive limit on the politics of change which can so easily appear to get out of control. Moreover, managing change effectively reduces anxiety and helps those who find change stressful to cope with as individuals. This in turn leads to a more positive attitude to change. Thus it is that we come full circle. If these ideas are synthesised in a managerial approach to organisational change then there seems to be a better prospect of success and effectiveness. Difficult and demanding in practice, these ideas are offered as the basis of how we can see changes through. The ideas presented here are summarised in Fig.7.4. The key point is that only by synthesising the management of transitions, dealing with organisational cultures and handling organisational politics constructively, can the environment be created in which creativity, risk-taking, learning and the rebuilding of self-esteem and performance can be achieved. If such a synthesis can be sustained, then learning and change can follow. More important, because people have learned about the business through the process of changing,

Fig. 7.4 Managing major changes.

the organisation will probably become more effective. By creating the conditions for extensive problem-solving and positive attitudes to change, future effectiveness is created. Maintaining the momentum for change then requires that the skills discussed here be further deployed to sustain effort. Team-building (see Adair 1986; and Belbin 1983), flexibility, being sensitive to needs, recognising good performance, managing the information to maintain credibility, rewarding people, sharing information and generating feelings of ownership, will all help to maintain the momentum. A case study is now presented to illustrate some of the points made in this chapter.

Case study: Reorganisation at EPD

EPD is the British manufacturing and marketing division of a European company we shall call International Electronics (IE). In 1974, EPD was a department of another subsidiary of IE sharing marketing, manufacturing, engineering, R&D, personnel and accounting facilities with other product groups in that subsidiary. When EPD production exceeded 50,000 units per week, it was separated off. Thirty-five thousand of the 50,000 units were electro-mechanical switches (relays) used in a wide range of machines (cars, domestic appliances, control gear, telephone exchanges). The growth of the telephone network had created a dramatic increase in the demand for relays. When EPD was formed, it had a number of long-term contracts including one with the Post Office (or the part of it now known as British Telecom) accounting for between 25,000 and 30,000 relays per week. At that time it was anticipated that within a decade all electro-mechanical and hybrid (part solid-state, using microprocessors) exchanges would be replaced by

System X, a fully solid-state system. Philips, Pye, STC, IBM, Plessey, GEC, Siemens, ITT, General Electric, Ericsson and Westinghouse had produced prototypes under test in Britain and elsewhere. At that point, however, solid-state technology presented significant technical problems and the question of when a reliable and stable solid-state system would be available was an open one.

In 1975, the Post Office's demand for EPD electro-mechanical relays increased dramatically to 45,000 per week. By the end of 1978, demand growth hit supply constraints, production being unable to meet demand of 70,000 units per week. To meet this and other anticipated growth, new production machines were developed during 1975-8, to be installed during 1979 (see Fig.7.5). By March 1979, output had been increased to 85,000 units per week, with the production development programme due to be put into effect during the summer.

Early in 1978 IE introduced a new management structure following the appointment of a new chief executive. Until 1978, all divisions (including EPD) had been managed with a significant degree of autonomy over pricing and output decision. Moreover, the group had managed with a participative/consultative style. By the late 1970s IE was experiencing increasing overseas competition in a period when higher R&D expenditure seemed essential to secure the group's future, not least in microprocessor development. Facing these liquidity and other pressures, the new chief executive

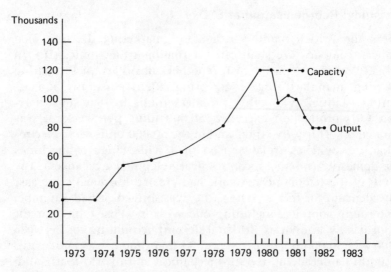

Fig. 7.5 Output/sales of electro-mechanical relays by EDP, 1973–80.

felt the need to achieve tighter central control over the divisions. Divisional general managers now reported to the group production director. Their line managers in accounting, engineering, marketing, personnel and sales reported functionally to the group.

The chief executive, previously finance director, had implemented a policy of trading 'up-market' which was very successful until 1980. EPD had raised prices ahead of inflation since the early 1970s, despite increased foreign competition. The EPD relay was priced higher than that of any of its rivals. EPD was able to offer continuity of supply, quick delivery, rapid replacement and high quality. British competitors manufactured to stock. EPD ran a multi-variant production line and delivered 98 per cent of output to target date. The new capacity, providing increased output from 85,000 units per week to 125,000 units per week, was installed by the end of 1979. Output of 122,000 units per week was achieved once in February 1980 and twice again in April 1980. The division was working three five-day shifts at that time. Along with the new capacity a new production incentive scheme was introduced, aimed at minimising lateness, absenteeism and extended breaktimes. Unit costs came down as a result of cuts in overtime. Quality circles, which EPD production management deplored, were organised by central group management. EPD management were concerned that these quality circles eroded production time and that the ideas emerging were not new, whilst the workforce felt that their ideas were being listened to and implemented.

In early 1980 IE reorganised corporate overheads allocation. There had been 'group management charges', 'central services' and 'site services'. 'Central services' had been allocated on the basis of the use made of services (training, research and development, selection and recruitment). Services were now to be charged as a fixed charge on capital employed in the business. Overheads charged to EPD increased immediately by 30 per cent. Also introduced was a monthly divisional target review meeting. This meeting was chaired by the chief executive and other members of the group board would attend. At the meeting divisional general managers would present actual performance compared to budgeted performance for their division over the last quarter.

In June 1980 British Telecom announced a major cutback in its modernisation and replacement programme, revising forward volumes downwards. Continuity of supply no longer mattered. Everyone, including customers, now had excess stocks. EPD charged £2.20 per standard relay; the lowest price on the market was £1.65. Priorities were changing dramatically but adjustment takes time.

EPD management felt that time was not on their side. Moreover, would electro-mechanical relays be needed when trade recovered?

EPD had invested in continuity of supply, reliability and quality. Customers now emphasised price. Demand fell back by 18 per cent by September 1980. EPD, under pressure from group management, reduced average prices to £2.00. Volume recovered by 6 per cent. A further cut to £1.90 with discounts depending on quantity and shipment frequency, was made. Volume recovered a further 3 per cent by March 1981.

The production development programme had been based on an assumption of long runs. There were now shorter runs with more downtime resulting from the need to reset machines between batches of different products. With income falling and costs increasing, the first 1981 divisional target review loomed large at the beginning of April 1981. The general manager of EPD was moved to another division of IE at the end of 1980, being replaced by the production manager, promoted to the new post of 'plant manager'. Marketing and sales were transferred to the group headquarters. These changes were made in all divisions of the group at that time. In December 1980 the personnel director of the UK group had been instructed to carry out a major redundancy programme in 1981, the target being 35 per cent of all employees. EPD had achieved

Table 7.1. The divisional target review, April 1981 (Extract)

EPD plant manager:	*Presents two charts showing performance below target.*
Chief executive:	OK.
Plant manager:	*Presents charts showing unit costs, stocks and headcounts all increased over last quarter.*
	Pause
Chief executive:	You need to take cost out of the product.
	Pause
	OK.
Plant manager:	*Shows another chart showing directs and indirects.* We have budgeted a 3% reduction on the next quarter.
Chief executive:	What does fifteen indirects mean?
Plant manager:	Four toolmakers and eleven setters.
Chief executive:	What do setters do?
Plant manager:	Split runs have increased changeovers. There are three per shift and one day man to carry over.
Chief executive:	You need to look harder at stocks and indirects. They need to come right down. OK?

significant progress in managing costs since 1978. In the new conditions short-term results, and a determined bid to survive became increasingly emphasised by the group. Moreover, group management were talking of the need to move from three shifts to two shifts or even single-shift working.

The chief executive calls for a reduction of costs associated with the manufacturing of relays. The plant manager responds by indicating his intention to reduce the employee total (direct and indirect) by 3 per cent in the next quarter. The chief executive then questions the total of indirects. The plant manager explains that each shift has one setter assigned to it, with an additional setter working day shift to deal with machine problems not dealt with by the shift setters. As is often the case, what is said tells only part of the story – the views left unstated may still have a powerful impact.

That afternoon the EPD plant manager held a management meeting in which the divisional target review outcomes were outlined. It was decided that one shift would be eliminated, and that the factory would go from a five-day week to two-shift four-day working, with overtime suspended and finished stocks to be cut by reduced output and by price cuts to increase sales volumes. To some extent his was a compromise decision, based upon the EPD plant manager's views regarding pricing strategy. Moreover, a number of improvement projects were accelerated, aimed at cutting cost and assembly time by design and/or materials change.

Despite the two-shift four-day week there was still excess capacity. If operations were reduced to single-shift working, indirect costs would become proportionately higher. This might lead to the reduction of indirect numbers – the skilled men needed to deal with machine setting, problems and improvement projects. The plant manager wished to reduce prices to give greater volume and longer runs, thus reducing downtime and costs. Group management accounting countered this with the argument that any savings would be offset by increased stock costs and tighter margins.

Group marketing forecast a 5 per cent decline in sales by July 1981. The group proposed a move to single-shift operation of five days, reduction in numbers of indirects, and expenditure limits (for example, expenditure on tooling to be reduced from £3,000 to £1,500 per week). The EPD plant manager resolved to implement the expenditure limits but to minimise redundancies. The options available to him to meet the group income target were as follows;

1. Increase selling price, accepting reduced demand but allowing for an increased transfer price to group marketing. This would allow him to work two shifts over a seven-day fortnight and to

claim a government grant for short-time working. Marketing would resist an increased transfer price because this might require an increased sale price. Whatever approach was adopted, this approach might reduce marketing net income. Group marketing was now assessed on net income at the divisional target review.

2. Accept the group package working day work (five-day week). This option involved redundancies and other savings, including reduced indirects and the elimination of shift premiums. The trades unions were ambivalent. Any number of jobs might be better than none. People on the shop floor felt that management had let them down. There would not be an official strike but there might be some unofficial action. This might be difficult to control and, ultimately, the group might intervene and close the plant down. In any event, the present problems were a consequence of having geared up to higher volume. This had reduced flexibility because the efficient utilisation of the new capacity required longer runs and higher volumes.

EPD management felt that very little account was being taken of the effect of activity levels. When operators see work running out they slow things down. Meeting the targets set by the group involved a degree of fine tuning not possible when people believed it was in their best interests to slow things down. However, the EPD plant manager was determined to create an impression of decisive action.

Negotiations to move to day working were begun in July 1981. The immediate response was hostile. The plant manager said that it was not negotiable and that a three-day week might become necessary. Union officials said that while they were 'sympathetic to local management's difficulties', they believed the plant and local management to be vulnerable to group pressures. Local management was 'on the run'. Day working was introduced in August 1981. It was agreed that redundancies would initially be handled through a voluntary scheme.

EPD management was now very concerned about the future of the plant. IE was pursuing microprocessor development work energetically, but in other divisions which possessed the relevant experience in solid-state technology. In the words of the production manager:

No one knows when relays will die. No doubt that when a solid-state device is good enough, they would close the plant down. The job would go to another division. No one is looking to see what else could be made in this plant. No one seems to know whose job it is to think about what to do when relays die. Group sales don't try hard enough to sell relays. When they are selling everything from fan heaters to computers, who wants to know about a boring relay?

In group marketing there were applications managers responsible for finding outlets for IE products. There was an applications manager for relays in 1982. EPD was beginning to produce a miniaturised relay. This device had been developed by the West German division of IE and met the space constraints of new exchange systems. It presented significant quality and manufacturing problems. The West German division had made significant progress in the development of the device and by 1980 had achieved an output of 10,000 units per week. Other EPD designs for switching devices were under review. The applications manager felt that the demand for the miniaturised relay might overtake the standard relay. However, he was concerned about the uncertainty surrounding the future of relays. All depended upon solid-state developments. The standard relay had outlived everyone's wildest dreams. 'It goes on and on and on. It's a gift.'

New product development at IE follows a fairly set pattern. Engineers in the divisions come up with a product idea. Marketing calculates volume potentials. These are then put to the new products committee, drawn from group management. If approved, the division will then be given the go-ahead for expenditure to develop and launch the product. Whilst the initiative comes from divisions, there is an ongoing interaction between people in the divisions and people at the group about new ideas, new product proposals and developments generally. Thus any specific new product proposal may have been the subject of such discussion and interaction for a considerable time before the division submits a formal proposal.

The reorganisation of the group introduced in 1978 aimed at achieving greater central control appears to have had a significant impact on the management of the group. From 1980 onwards there was increasing concern with the management of cost. But how rational is a process of management decision which ultimately turns its back on enterprise, development and growth? EPD has experienced dramatic change since the mid-1970s. To what extent have its attempts to manage cost conflicted with the management of change and innovation? What is the role of general management in such a tradition? What scope (or discretion) is available to divisional or group management to allow the introduction of changes aimed at improvement? What factors appear to bound or limit the scope for change?

Chapter 8

Managing through crisis

Introduction

The 1970s and 1980s have been an era of dramatic change affecting public and private organisations alike. They have also been an era in which companies have failed (that is failed to operate successfully in a marketplace and been liquidated or gone bankrupt) or contracted as previous levels of activity became unsustainable in one way or another. An early study of the causes and symptoms of 'corporate collapse' was published by Argenti (1976) with a more recent study being that of Kharbanda and Stallworthy (1986). It is clear enough that the onset of failure can be predicted and failure avoided through management actions. A number of such examples has recently generated a new genre of management book – the management of turnaround (Slatter 1986).

Elements in corporate failure

Argenti has summarised the key elements in corporate failure as follows:
1. Ineffective management. He specifically mentioned the failure to allow a strong enough sense of financial realism to pervade senior management discussion.
2. Accounting information. Failed organisations often have no cash-flow forecasts, no costing system, no system of budgetary control and have problems valuing assets.
3. Managers recognise but do not act on symptoms. The symptoms are recognisable but often only in a quantitative sense, for example, in the areas of quality, delays and poor maintenance.
4. Creative accounting. This is frequently associated with failure. Managers may refuse to believe the evidence and engage in 'creative accounting' in order to publish optimistic reports.

Argenti suggests that creative accounting is often a defence mechanism supporting a refusal to admit failure, rather than an act of fraud.

5. Overtrading. A firm's sales, stock levels and activity level generally increase faster than does the available capital. A cash-flow crisis can result.
6. Banks and gearing. High gearing can leave firms vulnerable.
7. The major project. Many organisations fail as a consequence of taking on a major project which proves financially, technically and managerially, beyond their resources.
8. The inability to adapt to changing circumstances (discussed elsewhere in this book).
9. Rescue. This is often possible because a viable core of business can remain.

Kharbanda and Stallworthy (citing an unnamed chief executive) suggest that failure is characterised by four stages:

1. Impulsiveness: to achieve growth targets management takes risks and seizes opportunities, expecting to consolidate later.
2. Stagnation: if a company has been successful, so 'why change'.
3. The 'headless' firm: divisions run largely autonomously with little central direction and leadership.
4. The aftermath: to turn the company, sizeable risks and dramatic actions are needed.

If the key elements of failure can be recognised, is it possible to predict the failure of any given organisation? Such a facility would clearly be useful. Some work has been done on the use of financial ratios. Perhaps the most influential is that of Altman *et al.* (1969). This work identifies a Z-score, which is a ratio based on working capital, total assets, cumulative retained earnings, sales, debt, market value of company, and earnings before tax and interests. Whilst the formula used is not uncontroversial, Altman suggests that if Z is less than 1.8 failure is certain, whilst if Z is more than 2.7 the company is almost certain not to fail − this is based on empirical studies of 'matched' companies (one which failed and one which did not). Whatever credence one can give to ratios, however complex, as predictors, it seems clear enough that 'signals' of failure can be observed before the fact, thus allowing prediction (see Argenti 1977).

Prevention or turnaround?

But what can be done? Organisations facing the problems we have outlined here must face a number of key challenges. They must achieve sustainable changes quickly but without the resources often available in periods of growth. They must reorganise and rationalise either at the level of the firm or, sometimes, at the level of the industry in order to cut overcapacity. Difficult decisions must be taken and implemented. Pulling out of traditional areas of activity is easier said than done. Building up new areas of activity may require new skills and new people. Redesigning products, updating processes and revitalising services takes massive effort. Taking advantage of new technologies quickly enough to capitalise on them is often a key issue. It must be done quickly enough to turn them to advantage but not so quickly that the firm becomes over-exposed with an ill-developed technology. For Bernard Taylor (1983) these challenges require a new style of management, incorporating a number of features:

Decisiveness
The situation calls for a speed of decision and ruthlessness in decision-making: a willingness to take unpleasant decisions and to face public criticism in order to ensure the continuation and recovery of the overall business.

Direct communication
Management must rely more on personal face-to-face meetings and telephone conversations, rather than on formal committees and paperwork systems.

Personal responsibility and accountability
There must be a greater emphasis at all levels on personal responsibility and accountability for meeting the targets and deadlines which are necessary if the business is to survive.

Central control of funds
This accountability is accompanied by a tighter central control of cash and an assumption by top management of the right to reallocate cash among divisions.

Investment and disinvestment
There is a need to re-think the future prospects for each product and market segment – in terms of the growth and profit potential and how to stay competitive in price, quality and service often on a lower level of business, and take radical decisions to invest or disinvest.

Expansion internationally
As growth slows down in traditional markets, it is necessary to expand internationally, sometimes into politically risky areas.

Personal negotiation
The restructuring and rationalisation which is taking place demands political skills of a high order and the ability to negotiate with employee representatives, with pressure groups, and with government bodies at home and abroad.

Innovation and risk-taking

There is a recognition that firms must adopt and develop the new technologies, or go under – introducing new products and processes and pioneering new businesses.

Management of turnaround

The key problem is to manage the contraction of traditional activities whilst at the same time expanding new activities. This must be achieved quickly and with limited resources, often under significant pressure from curious, demotivated staff and problems with the media. Turnaround strategies often include the following:

1. Mergers and co-operative supply, design or manufacturing/assembly agreements.
2. Sales of assets.
3. Programmes aimed at reducing overheads.
4. Improved systems of cost and budgetary control.
5. Value-for-money programmes.
6. Productivity improvement programmes including closing old-fashioned plant, concentrating on new facilities, automation, quality improvement, new technology.
7. Developing new corporate strategies.

Whilst 'turnaround' is often discussed in connection with private sector companies, it is worth noting that similar pressures have been faced in the public sector. Strategies for change in the public sector can include:

1. New systems of management (for example, the introduction of general management in the Health Service).
2. New strategies and approaches (for example, the development of commercialisation programmes and marketing in higher education).
3. New systems for human resource development (for example, appraisal systems in the education service).
4. Rationalisation simplification, automation and reorganisation (across organisations public and private).

The issues and challenges to be faced are similar in both the public and private sectors. As an example, one crucial area of improvement faced by organisations in both sectors is information systems, as the *Sunday Times* (6 September 1987) observed:

One specialist in the field ... a partner in Arthur Andersen and Co, management consultants, says he believes that the importance of information technology training was only now beginning to dawn on top executives in Britain.

The survey results confirmed what many of us had suspected – that many organisations are failing to realise that they are in the information technology business and that their future depends on their management understanding the technology.

Information technology, deployed effectively, can become a key, strategic resource, for example changes to budgeting, systems in health care towards decentralised budgetary control demands effective and decentralised provision of information.

So far the key elements of organisational failure have been examined and ways of managing crisis and turnaround briefly reviewed. At the outset it was suggested that crisis can be predicted. In fact it is now possible to go a stage further to suggest that a number of organisational 'syndromes' can be identified, each with strengths and weaknesses. These are listed with their major characteristics, the likely practical symptoms of the 'syndrome', the strengths and weaknesses of the syndrome and a typical example of that 'syndrome', in Table 8.1. Here it is suggested that a corporate failure has a long and identifiable history in each case: different in each case and a function of the specific organisation and its background, but identifiable.

Management and technology

It has been observed that the role of management in ensuring the timely and effective application of new technology is one of the key elements of turnaround management. In this concluding section of this chapter the reasons why this is so and some of the opportunities thus created will be examined.

Alvin Toffler (1970: 1980) argues that we still think about new technology as though it were simply a refinement of mechanistic technology, and this tunnel vision prevents its proper use. He points out three misconceptions:

1. Failure to appreciate feedback. Positive or negative feedback controls the speed and direction of new technology because they *are* the channels for interaction with social needs and values. Mechanistic thinking is aimed at producing more at a lower cost for a mass and non-discriminating market.
2. Seeing technological and scientific advances in isolation from each other. They should be seen as mutually reinforcing and beneficial, so as to understand that they usually only have real impact when developments converge, as with telecommunications and computers. This failure makes a nonsense of present

Table 8.1. Organisational syndromes.

Syndrome	Characteristics	Symptoms	Strengths	Weaknesses	Examples
Tight control	Distrust Analytical Centralised Reactive Sophisticated information systems	Incremental change 'Muddling through' Too much consultation Too many meetings Poor innovation	Good knowledge of threats and opportunities Diversification	Lack of clear strategy Insecurity	Dramatic loss of market or market share
Systems focus	Tight, formal controls Standardisation Hierarchical structures Conformity	Lack of innovation Ritual Low involvement Inflexibility Fixation	Efficient operations Well-integrated product-market strategy Distinctive competence	Traditional structures predominate Manager dissatisfied over lack of influence and discretion	Achievement of dominance from relatively weak position Frequent loss of control during history
Personal style	Highly centralised Unpredictable Inadequate structures Poor information systems	Unbridled growth Inconsistent strategy into and out of markets Decisions without analysis Little consultation	Change	Wasted resources Problems of control Inadequate role of second-level managers Rash expansion policies	Rapid growth, chief executive wishing to 'prove himself'
Paralysis	Lack of confidence Leadership vacuum Bureaucratic Hierarchical	Insular Decisions avoided Change difficult	Efficient internal operations Focused strategy	Limited to traditional markets Apathetic managers Weak competitive position	Well-established, same technology, customers and competition for many years
Leaderlessness	Leadership vacuum Power struggles	No involvement Incremental change Poor information flows Effective power in shifting coalitions of second-level managers	Creativity	Inconsistent strategy Lack of leadership Climate of distrust Poor co-operation	'Withdrawn' chief executive

Source: Adapted from Miller and De Vries (1985)

economic planning, trade policies, environmental safeguards and social legislation.

3. Assumptions that only large investments yield large results. Technological development is not a steady linear progression but rather a 'yeasty, seething, interactive process'.

The collection, analysis and distribution of information quickly and flexibly has made it a key economic resource. Its impact is not so much a change in principle as an explosion of scope and speed. However, this third computer-based information revolution produces a post-industrial economy so that understanding and using the new technologies both requires and confers power.

Why information is power

One definition of information technology sees it as the scientific, technological and engineering disciplines and the management techniques used in information handling and processing; their applications; computers and their interaction with men and machines; and associated social, economic and cultural matters. This definition illustrates the stress placed on links between technology and social and cultural patterns. That information is wealth is relatively easy to demonstrate. Examples of how knowing something enables cost reduction through better management and greater utilisation of resources abound. These practical examples also show the social/cultural impact of technology and our increasing ability to harness technology and make it work in specific ways. A Water Authority in the western UK has introduced computer control of water flows and pressures, increased accuracy of usage production, surveyed sewers and drains by remote camera and build up a data bank of information. This has allowed saving on four fronts:

1. Electricity consumption is reduced by matching pressure to real needs.
2. Wastage from leaks and bursts is minimised.
3. Personnel costs on maintenance and overtime emergency repair is reduced.
4. Capital expenditure is cut because of precise knowledge of needs.

The system can be used for planning work and aiding emergency decisions. The flexibility of micro-technology allows the use of distant sensors which relay information to a central processor and also of links between numbers of 'intelligent' terminals which process the information they collect and co-ordinate with other computers in their network.

Many of the examples show distribution or collection of information through networks:

1. Airline booking systems in real time which link 250 airlines world-wide.
2. Bank branches and 500 international connections linked by a financial network.
3. Divisions of corporations able to consolidate accounts or pinpoint deviations from local budgets.
4. Police links to database files to check ownership details or a suspect's identity.
5. Supermarket checkouts that inform stock control thus linking input and output from the shop.

Some of these need central processing, for example, the airline bookings, and some need a multitude of desktop processors, for example, the corporations and credit-card agencies. Timeshare computer systems are turning from their original function of processing at long distance with spare capacity to creation of information banks. Systems like ICL's Content Addressable File Store (CAFS) can access information on vague human questions by searching, thus eliminating the bottlenecks in indexed systems and the frustration of not knowing the exact question needed. The system works because of the speed with which new generation computers scan data.

What micro-electronics can do

Computers are cheap, small and fast enough to perform any task that human instructions can define. Thus man has the first *universal* machine, and it is a machine with no moving parts. The consequence is that today much wider areas of human labour can be taken over by micro-electronics. The jobs that disappear are not confined to the distasteful, laborious or dangerous. Computer design systems can perform, faster and usually better, most of the routine work of the draughtsman and designer; the skills of the printer have been automated, word processors concertina typing tasks and replace typing pools; the computer's ability to gather and analyse decision-framing information is changing the functions of middle management; computers that contain the distilled knowledge of leading specialists can affect the routine work of professionals from lawyers to university lecturers.

This ability would seem to support the argument that the onset of computers tends to take 'middle-man' jobs, reducing the need for people between the origins of products and end-users. This could apply to travel agents and bank officials as much as to semi-skilled manual workers. Briefly, greater wealth is being produced by fewer but much more highly-skilled people.

So far, new technology equals new wealth equals new demand equals new jobs but the process is accelerating and people would appear to have to retrain several times; as they are deskilled they will have to be reskilled. The computer – this new universal machine – does seem to alter the base equation because new areas of mass employment can so quickly become automated in turn. This is very much the pattern in manufacturing industry.

Changes in service industries

In the same way that technological changes in agriculture reduced the number of people needed to work on the land, technological change has reduced the numbers required so that the service industry has progressively taken over from manufacturing and production as the main employer. However, while expanding the service sector and producing greater wealth, micro-electronics is not increasing employment. This need not mean greater general unemployment provided we find a way to:
(a) replace or change our social and personal priorities;
(b) concentrate on creating wealth and simply jobs;
(c) use that wealth to create opportunities for recreation, education and community and public service.

Concluding comment

These then are some of the issues to be faced in managing technology. Doing so in crisis or turnaround situations adds to the complexity although not necessarily the difficulty (in the short term at least). Crisis can concentrate minds and energy! This chapter has considered some of the means to be adopted in crisis situations. Elsewhere in the book the strategies and skill appropriate to managing changes such as new technology are examined. Here both crisis and new technology have been seen as sources of challenge to management.

Chapter 9

Small business management

Introduction

What is a small business? The notion of size is arbitrary and therefore a concise definition is impossible. It could be argued that whether a business is small or large is dependent upon the number of employees or the amount of profit generated, total sales, or one of any number of other measurements. Perhaps a better means of definition can be found in identifying common characteristics. Storey (1973) outlines a set of such characteristics. These are that a small business usually has a small market share, that normally it is managed by the owners and that the owners are legally independent in taking decisions. Operating from a single establishment, it either makes or supplies a single product or a small number of closely-related products. Generally it operates in a local market, though there will obviously be exceptions.

Many see small business as one of the 'engines of growth' in the economy. Entrepreneurs create new businesses to exploit new business opportunities. Fast-growing small firms generate employment. These views are not without their critics. However, it can certainly be said that small businesses are an important part of the economy and that managers in small businesses need many skills. This chapter will consider some of the issues facing managers setting up and running small businesses and the role of the entrepreneur. Whilst some of what is said must be set within the UK legal and institutional context, this will be kept to a minimum, partly for the non-UK reader, partly because the situation is changing all the time, partly because many excellent detailed books are available. Here it is intended merely to give an overview.

The role of the small business

According to Storey (1973), small firms can be characterised as follows:

1. They provide a form of competition to larger firms in that particular sector thereby acting as a moderator in price raising, or have the support function of being able to provide 'one-offs' which large businesses cannot accommodate.
2. They can be seen as the potential large corporations in the future.
3. They generally provide intimate harmonious work environments where owners and employers are on familiar terms. This tends to lead to fewer industrial disputes and reduced absenteeism.
4. They can be used as a means of regenerating employment in deprived areas.
5. By nature they need to be innovative and flexible in order to operate.

It is easy to find many exceptions to these factors but making some attempt at identifying features contributes to an understanding of some of the issues and problems small businesses do experience.

The survival and growth of small businesses

During the last century the small business has shown a tremendous capacity to harness itself to industrial change and provide a necessary appendage to industry at large. An example of this capacity is the British firm Twyfords. The advent of public health in the UK led to improved sanitation. This led companies such as Twyfords to produce a whole range of sanitary equipment, baths, toilets, and so on. This in turn led to the refurbishment of homes, providing work for builders, plumbers, and others, which in its turn led to a need for drains to be built and maintained. A huge number of small business enterprises have sprung up to meet this challenge.

However, the other side to this optimism are the difficulties small businesses experience. Small businesses often feel they get a poor deal in the grand scale of things – that governments ignore their needs by concentrating on policies to aid large corporations whilst being insensitive to the needs of small companies and their importance in terms of the total economy. The introduction of Value Added Tax is a suitable example of this. It was implemented as a means of collecting taxes by an easier method than that of purchase tax. To the small businesses it has meant increased paperwork and has become an irritating burden and strain on them – as they see it, the government has made *them* tax collectors.

In the history of a successful small business there comes a point at which it needs or has the potential to grow. Often a back-street business will move from its old premises onto an industrial estate in order to meet the increased demand for its product. A frequent and unfortunate consequence of this is the inability to recognise that former business practices will no longer be appropriate to the new situation, and that a shift in emphasis on functions will be necessary. Modern business is a complex issue. Growth brings with it new responsibilities and problems. The small businessman is not usually equipped with the management skills which he needs once his business grows beyond certain limits. He cannot afford to devote all his time to the mixed bag of issues he once dealt with and is in danger of being swamped by day-to-day detail. An awareness of this issue is essential – an adaptable and flexible attitude is needed. Strength comes from adjusting to situations and accepting that new, more sophisticated techniques are required.

The small business owner must be aware of the specific peculiarities of his firm and develop techniques to meet the needs of his business. Small businesses are vulnerable and susceptible to technological and environmental changes. Because they are small, such changes will have a greater impact upon their health. Being sensitive to this can result in being able to react and adapt to changes quickly.

Planning ahead is obviously a key issue in the survival of the small business. Decisions have to be made which will have both long-term and short-term consequences. Therefore it follows that improving decision-making will reduce the risk of failure and promote potential growth. Decisions tend to be made as short-term strategies to overcome current problems. For example, a product is in danger of becoming obsolete and so survival becomes the maxim. In these circumstances long-term ramifications may be overlooked as every effort is devoted to finding a suitable replacement product. So, although the decision may cope with short-term survival, it will affect the long-term growth of the business. However, the majority of decisions are not as profound as this.

Growth is not always seen as a survival tactic, too often it is directly seen to relate directly and singularly to sales. What the small business needs to appreciate is that sales growth, though important, is only one aspect of the overall company profile. Filling order books with future sales may appear a visible, attractive solution but it must be related to the type of customer it represents. If a high proportion of these orders are slow payers or bad debtors then a cash gap will result. The financial health of a small business is dependent upon closely related factors of which sales growth is only one and if too much emphasis is placed on this function the company's survival will be put at risk.

The objective of the company is to make a profit but not all profits are necessarily in the form of cash. In small businesses two other factors need particular attention to assist a healthy cash flow. These are debts and stocks. Accounts receivable or 'debts' form part of a company's assets. However, the length of time it takes to realise these debts needs serious consideration. The older the debt, the less attractive its value becomes – therefore the pace at which these debts are cleared is an important feature in the health of small businesses. A small business must understand the crucial nature of its debts. Accounts which are cleared quickly are healthier than larger, long-term debts which cannot be readily realised and block the flow of money circulating through the business. The other important feature affecting cash flow which needs addressing is the amount of stock held and what that stock is doing. The balance between raw materials, work in progress and the amount of finished goods must be understood and managed in order to control stock and prevent assets being tied up too long which will in turn affect the company's liquidity. It was noted earlier that decisions which affect survival can be potentially dangerous to long-term growth and likewise decisions affecting liquidity need a high priority as it not only affects growth but productivity. Small businesses are particularly susceptible to cash-flow problems because they rarely use cash controls and so any decision which affects cash flow is directly related to the company's liquidity.

So, to summarise, growth cannot simply be related to sales volume. Growth occurs in small businesses when it can improve the quality of its earning by increasing turnover and/or eliminating low profit areas, thus increasing its liquidity in a way which does not have a decreasing effect on other areas.

Time management

The effective use of time is crucial to the success of the small business. It is compounded in the small business because of the pressure on a small number of people to perform all the functions of the company which in large organisations would be carried out by experts with a back-up staff. The small businessman has to cope with sales, accounts, purchasing and other functions, albeit on a smaller scale than the large organisation. He may be required to have skills which he altogether lacks. As a small business grows, its owner will constantly face the problems of being involved in the operational side of the business and managing it. The small business man needs to be aware of the business environment and social demands of the community on top of the day-to-day running, planning and managing. Success depends on three elements, according to Cohn and Lindberg (1974): selflessness, individualism and meticulousness. Selflessness is the objectivity needed to make company-orientated decisions. Individualism assures advantage to the firm because of the foresight and courage needed to make decisions. Meticulousness is following the decisions through.

Sufficient time must be devoted to these factors and so the small business man must learn to treat time as a finite resource – an asset, the appropriate utilisation of which provides the key to successful management. Managers of small businesses appear to have little control over their time – they are subjected to customers, employees and suppliers. Life becomes a barrage of telephone calls, people calling in to the office, dealing with post, and so on. Being too busy often becomes an excuse for appearing effective. Time must be planned and managed in order to gain maximum efficiency. Activity analysis is a simple way of investigating the use of time. Over a specified period – say, two weeks – a log is kept of what is done in each quarter-hour of the day. This will provide an individual breakdown of the time devoted to the various business activities and the opportunity to correct any perceived imbalances and improve time management. If the analysis reveals a large amount of time spent making decisions, for example, then delegation should be considered. Often decisions are of a common, repetitive nature, for example, holiday arrangements, time off, and advances in pay. These decisions could be dealt with more efficiently if an appropriate structure were implemented, thus releasing the manager to utilise his time usefully. In essence, the manager of a small business which is experiencing growth must use his time to *manage* and not simply to *do* more. His time needs to be directed towards providing products, services, cutting costs and creating a satisfying work environment for employees. General housekeeping functions must be delegated to others appropriate for the task. He needs to plan ahead, to organise and delegate in a way which leaves him free to attend to the more appropriate business of running the company, rather than letting the company run him.

The entrepreneur: characteristics

The notion of individual success and failure characterised in entrepreneurism has been a source of interest and fascination for man. In the entrepreneur we see bold individualism striving for success in the environment. What compounds the fascination is that the story rarely ends when he had 'made it'; success is often followed by failure. Therefore entrepreneurial 'sagas' continue to be of interest. Entrepreneurs are 'one-offs'; exceptions to the rule – deviants. For them the environment is turbulent, controlled by individuals who need to control and structure and so he or she activates a rebellious spirit as a means to demonstrate his need to break out and prove his independence. The juxtaposition of success and failure which now exists for the entrepreneur requires a certain resilience and awareness that he may have to restart again and again when disappointment occurs. De Vries (1980) describes the entrepreneur as 'creative destructive' – highly complex and creative and not the automaton which economists often like to believe his is. For De Vries, he is not that 'lightning calculator of pleasure and pain' and cannot resemble a mechanical creature of economic theory. Instead the entrepreneur is the active individualist exhibiting inconsistencies and confusions out of his motives, desires, outcomes – a person who lives under stress, who confronts us by what we perceive as irrational, impulsive behaviour. It is for these reasons that he cannot be fitted to the economists' rational, logical schemes. The entrepreneur is the person who conceives of an idea and implements this idea. He therefore needs to fulfil functions through this process, namely innovation, management co-ordination, and risk-taking.

So, how do we identify entrepreneurs? Studies appear to indicate that entrepreneurs exhibit a high level of achievement motivation, a need for autonomy and independence, and a risk-taking capacity. Power motivation appears to vary according to circumstance and leadership style and they often show a neglect of interpersonal relations, being more 'inner-directed'.

Finally, a high degree of aesthetic sense also appears to be a feature which contributes to the ability to consider off-beat combinations. There is diversity within entrepreneurial types. Smith (1969) describes two types of entrepreneur – the craftsman and the opportunist. Characteristics of the craftsman entrepreneur are limited education and training, low social awareness, and limited orientation to time. The opportunistic entrepreneur, however, shows wide education and training, high social awareness and an orientation towards the future. These two ideal types are then matched to type of firm, one being rigid, the other adaptive. The craftsman entrepreneur builds rigid structures within the firm, whereas the opportunistic entrepreneur creates a more adaptive, flexible structure. This is, of course, dependent to a large extent on the product and production methods. Although Smith could be criticised for oversimplicity, he does provide a framework within which to explore different types of entrepreneur. De Vries (1980) concludes from this that we may be producing a 'new breed' of entrepreneur, one which is better educated, less impulsive and more adaptive. He puts forward the suggestion that the impact of this 'new breed' could have powerful consequences on large bureaucratic organisations, preventing organisational decay and inertia, by providing an educated adaptive entrepreneurial input.

The entrepreneurs pass through a process of acceptance by wider society before being recognised. They often begin careers by a succession of job changes as they consistently seek careers and organisations willing to accommodate their ideas. They are often perceived by others as provocative, irritating and irrational. Researchers of entrepreneurism refer to this as the non-conformist stand and this behaviour is seen in a wider social context as disruptive and uncontrollable. In turn the entrepreneur experiences frustration and tension. For him the 'hunch' is the final conclusion at this stage. There is a lack of logical objectivity and reflectiveness. Analytical thinking and positive actions are seen to inhibit the creative flow.

From this stage of dissatisfaction, frustration and powerlessness, the entrepreneur passes on to high risk-taking behaviour. He becomes proactive in style, rejecting passivity and exercising control. He has experienced the frustration of trying to fit into structured environments and seeks out situations where he can control and be central to action. However, significant achievement has not been met and a paradox exists. Now the enterprise becomes the platform, the organisation the end of the road. A feature of entrepreneurial organisation is the dependency which the entrepreneur has created between himself and the work environment. Such enterprises are characterised by autocratic styles. Decision-making centres around the entrepreneur. His control is paramount and is identified with a lack of delegation, impulsive decision-making, successive changes in strategy. The entrepreneur finds it difficult to divorce himself from the day-to-day running of the organisation and move on to long-term strategic planning. Priorities are confused and disproportionate amounts of time are spent on trivia. This creates a highly unstable and uncertain organisational environment with a highly charged atmosphere. What is 'in' today can easily be 'out' tomorrow.

The organisational shape can be likened to a wheel with the entrepreneur at the centre, with subordinates feeling confused and dependent. Formal information systems are virtually useless and standard procedures non-existent. Responsibilities are blurred and highly subjective. The situation is ambiguous and stressful. Now the entrepreneur enters the danger zone. The qualities needed initially to create a constructive environment and lead to growth are in danger of being the tools for its own destruction. The time-scale of this will vary, but eventual financial losses usually become the indicator that change is essential if the organisation is to grow.

At this stage abdication is often the only alternative. The entrepreneur needs something new to invest his talent and energies into. But from an emotional point of view this is difficult and succession becomes a problem. Many examples exist where the son steps into the father's shoes and is followed by resentment and rivalry from other contenders. Now the entrepreneur and the organisation are no longer the primary power sources. Bankers, directors and customers now form powerful interest groups and the strength of the entrepreneur is diffused. His influence is diluted. A time of reassessment and realisation needs to be recognised. De Vries (1980) terms this 'entrepreneurial maturity'. There is a need to show willingness to assess strengths and weaknesses and move forwards in an individual sense. Frequently the only alternative for organisational survival becomes involuntary separation and represents the depressive feature of entrepreneurism. De Vries (1980) says:

While the entrepreneurial spirit is one of the strong countervailing forces preventing decay and decline of the economy as a whole, in the final deliberation the entrepreneur pays an extremely high price in an emotional sense in this process of economic growth.

It is clear that entrepreneurs exist both in corporate structures and in small businesses. How can this be accounted for? What are the differences? Bruce (1976) distinguishes entrepreneurial types and this is useful as it helps us to categorise and understand how different entrepreneurial types are utilised in organisations. He describes two basic types: the independent entrepreneur and the modal entrepreneur. There is evidence to support the theory that life experiences, social background and education explain which of these two categories an entrepreneur will belong to.

The independent entrepreneur

Independence is a powerful motivating force in all entrepreneurs. The independent entrepreneur has a strong desire to control his destiny and determine directly the fate of a commercial enterprise by exercising control. He is top dog. What is the social significance of this? The independent entrepreneur seeks out situations where he can express himself through his business and thereby achieve independence. In a sense society can view this as insurrection, it becomes almost an act of revolution not in a political sense but in an individual sense. Here lies a paradox. The entrepreneur kicks against career norms, his job hops seem without direction. However, once his desires find the appropriate environment and talent has an avenue to express itself, then he is seen as a vital part of the economy, providing innovation and becoming a valuable part of society. At this point the successful entrepreneur is applauded; he is no longer a threat but an economic safety valve.

Bruce subdivides the independent entrepreneur into the elite and the ubiquitous entrepreneur. The elite entrepreneur is in a sense the 'ultimate' entrepreneur. His need for independence drives him to private enterprise. He begins with a small company, it grows and continues to grow into a large corporation. The ubiquitous entrepreneur begins with a small company; this remains a small company as it lacks the capacity for growth. As he puts it: 'There is a difference in both attitude of mind and ability between the individual who runs the local grocery store and the individual who has built up a chain of them'.

The modal entrepreneur

The modal entrepreneur fits more easily into business environments. Typically he is employed by large organisations and is responsible to the board of directors. He runs the organisation because he is employed to do so, whereas the independent entrepreneur runs his company because he chooses to.

Role deterioration

Discontinuity between the individual's perception of self and the roles held in society is a characteristic of the typical entrepreneur which results in role deterioration – the individual being no longer able to fulfil the role. This can happen in a variety of ways due to circumstances – when we experience the death of someone close to us, a loss of job. Such experiences have a significant impact on our lives and to a large extent force us into change of some type. Attitudes have been forced to change, reassessment takes place, roles need to be modified, old behaviours are no longer appropriate and need to be updated to fit new situations. Important decisions have to focus and find new direction; past and future interface.

Bruce (1976) suggests that role deterioration is a characteristic of entrepreneurs in that at some point in their career a determining event occurs which acts as a catalyst and some action is needed to resolve this conflict. Socially marginal individuals experience role deterioration by reason of their independent nature and often unconventional solutions are the means of resolving this conflict. This, as Bruce suggests, may provide an explanation for the entrepreneurial spirit.

Corporate evolution

In a fascinating and readable book, Lloyd (1986) predicts that small, high-technology companies will replace giant corporations as the dominant form of organisation. He goes on to suggest means of supporting these developments, arguing that even if this transition is inevitable, we should be concerned to achieve it as quickly as possible. There are, he suggests, a number of problems, particularly in the United Kingdom, as follows:

1. Entrepreneurs tend to be 'loners'. People who break away from larger businesses tend to operate on their own. There seems to be a reluctance to part with equity. This can mean that they lack management and financial support.
2. Large companies seem to create systems of benefits 'locking' people into their system. Pensions are perhaps the obvious case in point – hence the current interest in 'portable' pensions.
3. We have already discussed 'role models'. Lloyd follows many in bewailing the anti-business culture in the UK. However, there seems to be evidence of change for the better here.
   He comes to the conclusion 'that entrepreneurs are unemployable. They do not like working for others; they find the politicking ... irksome ... They seem to have a stronger sense of self than most. They are less risk-averse than average. They often become quite lonely. They need confidant(e)s and gurus from time to time'.
   Entrepreneurs also seem to be people capable both of vision and action (see Kingston 1977). They generate new ideas but cannot see them through to reality. They attract other people, attract their imagination and support. But most of all they need an institutional setting which is supportive and a rewarding culture. These views are not uncontroversial; however, they are lacking in practical guidelines.

New venture strategies

What should people running large corporations do if Lloyd's theory proves to be valid? He points to the present tendencies towards decentralisation which have already been referred to in this book. Divisions are given more autonomy. Often business units are identified and given substantial autonomy in the belief that if they are freed from the constraints presented by headquarters, they will be more innovative and more productive. However, Lloyd argues for a more active approach. Potential entrepreneurs within an organisation should be identified and supported. Where possible, teams of people with the relevant mix of skills should be put together and invited to set up their own company under the umbrella of the larger organisation, perhaps on the understanding that success will lead to a flotation, the larger parent retaining a significant equity stake. The parent should not, however, insist on retaining control. Motivation is important here. Control by the parent seems likely to reduce motivation. Many refer to this as the 'federal' organisation.

Lissem (1986) provides us with a different vision of how to develop the entrepreneurial spirit in companies, using ideas which enable us to link the ideas presented in this chapter. He refers to 'metapreneurs'. How are they to be developed? He suggests a number of practical ideas. At the core of his ideas lie the notions of how to enable change and how to manage for development. These ideas are worth pursuing in Lissem's own work. It seems that we need to both create the circumstances of challenge *and* provide appropriately supportive learning environments if entrepreneurial activity is to flourish.

Case study: Grant Electronics

John Grant is the founder, principal shareholder and managing director of Grant Electronics. He formed his company in 1965 after three years spent working in manufacturing for an electronics company. Grant Electronics was originally in the business of selling electric and electronic components to manufacturers of all types of office equipment. For the first three years the company acted largely as agents, using John Grant's charm, business flair and hard work to persuade small manufacturers to meet the specifications of large organisations which lacked the capacity to satisfy their needs from within. By the late 1960s it was becoming increasingly difficult to find firms with the skill or the willingness to undertake unusual

jobs, and the company gradually started the manufacture of proto-
type components which were highly complex in their specification
and were needed in relatively low numbers. This was a highly
profitable operation: so few people wanted this work that there
was virtually no ceiling to the prices the company could charge.

By 1970 Grant Electronics had six gifted electronic engineers
with great skill in developing new components and in adapting
existing components to make them more effective, more reliable
and easier to manufacture. Several patents were taken out, and other
manufacturers were licensed to manufacture in large quantities on
payment of royalty. These licences were only issued when the
capacity of Grant Electronics (which started manufacturing in 1969)
was fully stretched. For many years Grant Electronics has succeeded
in staying ahead of the market, always moving to a new product
before the large organisations tooled up to manufacture in such
quantity as to undercut the Grant Electronics price.

Today, Grant Electronics has a total workforce of 119 people; its
organisation chart is set out in Fig. 9.1. The premises are situated
in an outer London suburb with good access to public transport,
motorways and Heathrow Airport. They were bought for £100,000
in 1968 and have been modernised and fitted up to a high standard.
Most plant and equipment has been fully depreciated. The current
market value of this total asset is estimated conservatively at £1.5
million, assuming a buyer were available.

All employees, except for the salesmen, work at these premises.
Most of the production workers live locally. Their average length
of service is 12 years, and although the company has consistently
paid generous salaries, many of these people continue to live in
council property, having chosen not to go for home-ownership.

With very few exceptions, the senior employees have been with
the company since John Grant formed it. They have grown up with
the company and identify closely with it. 'Staff turnover, over the
years, has always been exceptionally low.'

The company has been a happy place to work; small enough for
everybody to know everybody else and for communication to be
open and easy. The employees at all levels feel that they contribute
to the success of the company, and that their contribution is
recognised through the excellent benefits package and a profit-
sharing scheme which John Grant introduced in 1978. Under that
scheme all employees qualify for a share in 25 per cent of the
annually declared profit. Individual shares are determined by reference to length of service and to effort and contribution as assessed
by the six members of the Employee Participation Committee. Since

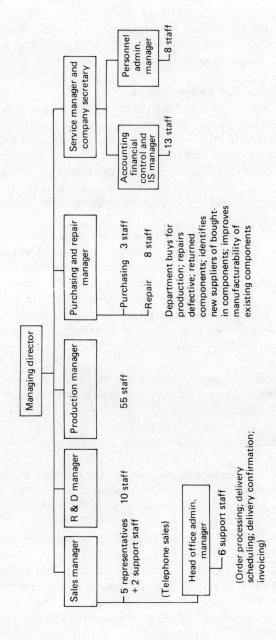

Fig. 9.1 Grant Electronics.

its inception six years ago this scheme has worked well and without any serious complaints from employees. Last year (1984), the average salary of £9,500 was boosted by an average profit-share bonus of £900. This was £125 less than the previous year. While there are no tangible signs of declining morale, John Grant knows that about 20 people are less satisfied now than they have been in the past, and that there is some sympathy for the unionisation of employees and formally negotiated wage settlements.

John Grant feels the time has come to take stock of his personal position. He is 45 and proud of having achieved so much in 20 years. He knows all his employees and counts some of them as friends. His sense of responsibility towards them is strong. He would like to expand his business, gain increased personal job satisfaction and realise his unfulfilled potential. He wants to exercise the power within him and create something durable which he could be proud of in his old age.

These ambitions are somehow frustrated by two contradictory factors. On the one hand, the obvious success of Grant Electronics has allowed a degree of complacency to creep in; on the other hand, there are signs that the firm's success and profitability are at risk. John Grant cannot seem to motivate corrective action because of the complacency. He cannot expand where he is, but how can he move to larger premises with so many employees unable and/or unwilling to move house? He cannot afford to do nothing while profits erode.

He knows that his business has to change and he recognises that there are many choices. Some of these choices – but not all – are listed below.

1. Sell out and find a new business venture.
2. Adapt his present company to secure long-term growth and profitability. But how?
3. Pay off employees unwilling to move, and transfer to larger premises in East Anglia where he could expand all aspects of his current business and bring down unit costs through increased manufacture, lower overheads and higher productivity.
4. Expand the R&D business. (But how long before competitor's R&D undercuts Grant Electronics?)
5. Expand the repair side of the business – the manager in charge sees this as a highly profitable growth area if Grant Electronics were to choose to recruit about 40 top-quality engineers to provide the service that office equipment customers cannot get from their suppliers.
6. Close the repair side of the business – it was set up initially to

ensure customer satisfaction but the contribution its eight staff can make is now questionable, and as presently organised this group is not contributing to profit. The eight employees have all been with Grant Electronics for a long time. They are not suitable for any other type of work now being done in the company.

7. Face the fact that Grant Electronics may not be able to manufacture profitably in the long term against competition and run down the production side of the business. But then what replaces the manufacturing contribution to cash flow and profit?

John Grant senses but cannot quantify changes in his workforce. He knows his profitability is declining, especially because of the cost of repair work and because of the low cost of competitive products. He could expand R&D but wonders if it is a business he wants to be in, suspecting that large R&D organisations become unmanageable.

Here we have a classic problem of business growth and success. In part the company now needs a more professional management approach. Part of the answer lies in examining the role of John Grant. He is a business man, a doer of deals. He is not effective in dealing with the day-to-day problems of managing the business. Can we create a business development function for John Grant to lead, perhaps as managing director, appointing others to handle the control of major functions? What about a management buyout? Whatever happens, John Grant is central to the company and, therefore, central to the problem. This is generally the case with small business management problems.

Chapter 10

The wider impact of organisations

In an increasingly complex business environment companies and organisations interact in a variety of ways. The decisions made by people in organisations also have an impact on the wider community. Whether we are concerned with product safety, environmental pollution, consumer protection, employment policies or other matters we are concerned with aspects of the relations of organisations with society.

This chapter will examine four related topics as follows:

1. Relationships between organisations and society, primarily to identify the main areas of concern and to consider the question of social responsibility.
2. The stakeholder model, considered as a model of organisational decision-making and adaptation.
3. The relationship between organisations as an increasingly important aspect of managerial work.
4. The notion of 'corporatism', a model of how the state sets out to influence organisations.

Relations between the organisation and society

That business firms and other organisations interact with their environments in ways which are considered by many outsiders to be of importance, is accepted by all. A number of these relationships are listed in Table 10.1. Similarly we might identify a set of interactions between a public sector organisation and its environment. For example, all of these interactions would clearly apply to a water authority. Most, perhaps all, and other besides would apply to a health authority.

Few people today hold to the view that the sole justification of business enterprise is to generate profits, although this may remain the most crucial objective of the business. It seems sensible to avoid

Table 10.1. Relations between a business and society.

---

1. *Consequence of the sale of goods and services.*
   Pricing.
   Advertising and expectations.
   After-sales support: parts and service.
   Continued availability of the product.
   Product safety.
   Environmental consequences.
   Social and cultural impact.

2. *Use and consumption of physical resources.*
   Scarce resources.
   Exhaustible resources.

3. *Use of people as resources.*
   Exposure to dangerous materials/noise/living and working conditions/disease/discrimination.
   Job security/career paths/jobs design and employee rights/mobility/education and training/redundancy and dismissal procedures.

4. *Waste from the operations of the firm.*
   Impact of waste on the environment.
   Dumping.
   Liquid wastes/poisoning/dumping into ocean.
   Sold waste/hand fill/value recovery.
   Discharges into air.
   Noise.
   Nuclear waste.

5. *Impact of the firm on the local community.*
   Use and support of community services.
   The 'one-company town' dependence.
   Hiring practices.
   Treatment of suppliers.
   Use and support of local colleges.

---

oversimplification. It is hard to accept the view that a business exists solely for the benefit of the shareholders, suppliers, employees, customers, its bankers, the local community, or the government. Similarly, it seems increasingly difficult to say that the sole justification of a public sector organisation is to be found in public service. One approach to this area is provided by the 'stakeholder' model described below.

The 'stakeholder' model

It is comparatively rare today for the senior management of large business organisations to proclaim that the maximisation of profits is their sole aim. It is more likely that objectives such as 'survival' or 'growth' will be emphasised. Profits are then regarded as a means to these ends; as a means of maintaining independence from external groups and institutions, and as a means of financing future organisational activity and growth. Profitability, survival and growth are therefore closely related. This has been recognised for many years in the management literature, which has stressed the separation of ownership from control in large firms and hence the need for the management group to satisfy the interests of other groups, such as shareholders, who may otherwise threaten the independent viability of the organisation and hence the position of the incumbent management group. Profits, being the difference between revenue (directly derived from the satisfaction of consumers) and costs (which are directly related to the rewards and employees and other suppliers of inputs), are traditionally identified with the interests of shareholders.

But the survival and viability of an organisation may in particular circumstances be threatened by the actions of any of these groups, although traditional company law recognises only the right to action by shareholders. All these groups, it has been argued, have a 'stake' in the success of the enterprise and hence may seek to protect or enhance this 'stake' by appropriate action, for example, strike action by employees, and either direct action by consumers or suppliers, or the lobbying of government to act on their behalf, for example, by the use of anti-monopoly policies. In practice, therefore, management has long recognised the need to pursue policies towards all 'stakeholders' which it is hoped will ensure the long-term viability of the enterprise, although traditional company law recognises the requirement to act only in the interests of shareholders.

Associated with this new 'stakeholder' concept is the argument that the growth of the organisation will be consistent with the needs of all stakeholders. This view may be characterised (in an admittedly oversimplified way) along the following lines. In order to grow, the organisation requires increased demand by consumers and an increased supply of finance to augment productive capacity to satisfy that demand. The successful firm will allow policies designed to increase demand by making existing products more attractive to consumers of by seeking out new demands and markets which will grow in the future. Only if these marketing policies are successful will the firm generate extra revenue, and marketing will be successful only if consumers continue to be satisfied.

If past policies have been successful the organisation will have generated profits, some of which will be paid as tax, some of which will provide finance for investment, and some of which will be distributed to shareholders. That portion which goes to the Exchequer will help pay for social services and other provisions which the government deems to be 'in the public interest'. That portion of profit which is paid out in dividends aims to satisfy shareholders. If shareholders are not satisfied, it is argued that they will either sell their shares or protest at the annual meeting, both of which could mean a possible change of management. On the other hand, those shareholders who have a preference for future capital gain could acquiesce to a lower payout policy and more profit retained for investment. Moreover, a good profit record could attract additional funds from the capital market which could supplement retained profit to finance new investment. In so far as productive capacity is extended, employment opportunities are enhanced either by more jobs and/or higher productivity and wages. The larger the organisation, the more career opportunities and rewards are available to management and the greater is the market provided to the suppliers.

In short, the argument is that the growth of the business enterprise benefits all 'stakeholders' – consumers, shareholders and investors, employees, government, management and suppliers. Moreover, the new 'stakeholder' orthodoxy can to a certain extent also be regarded as having adaptive capacities, as 'stakeholders' values and expectations change. For it may be argued that these will be reflected in their changed expectations of the organisation's performance, and may thus affect the terms on which they will be prepared to support the enterprise. If consumers' expectations of product performance change, for example, management would have to modify their product policy in order to maintain or increase the demand for their products. Similarly, if the attitudes of employees to the work environment changed, it could be argued that management's policy towards production systems and work organisation would have to be adapted in order to meet workers' new expectations, and thereby to maintain or increase productive efficiency. Thus in order to pursue the objectives of survival, profitability and growth, the new 'stakeholder' orthodoxy propounds that management must balance the interests of all stakeholders and seek to adapt to their changed expectation when the need occurs.

In practice, the acceptance of such a view requires the acceptance by management of wider responsibilities. But how can a reasonable balance between the various stakeholder groups be maintained? In this complex area can we develop a meaningful concept of 'social responsibility'? In a thoughtful book on this area, Beesley and Evans (1978) see social responsibility as a matter of how far a company deals with its environment by incorporating external concerns into its decision-making processes. It can do this on various levels:

1. Passive adaptation to the requirements of the environment, including adherence to the law, to the demands of powerful interest groups (for example, government), and to custom and practice.
2. Awareness of external concerns and a broad commitment to justify the company's actions.
3. Bargaining with important interest groups in the company's environment. This may involve altering policies to satisfy their requirements.
4. Incorporating external concerns as concerns of the company. This involves an active search for response to these concerns rather than merely regarding them as constraints on social activity.

Inter-organisational relations

All organisations have dealings with, and must take account of, other organisations. Organisations represent concentrations of resources (materials, personnel, specific expertise, information, finance) which managers cannot ignore. In the construction industry the contractor–subcontractor relationship is a classic case of an inter-organisational relation. There are a number of reasons which may cause a business to subcontract, including the need to obtain special items; the need to obtain access to special knowledge and skills; and the need to augment the resources of the business in a period when they would otherwise be overloaded. Inter-organisational relations of this type are basically human relations with legal obligations and responsibilities involved. To be properly understood, however, these relations must be analysed in terms of the relative power of the parties concerned. The relation between a contractor and a subcontractor is one of exchange and dependence. The contractor depends upon the subcontractor for the performance of certain tasks by a certain time and to a set of standards and specifications. The subcontractor may depend upon the contractor as a source of business and continuity. Similar relationships develop between suppliers of raw materials, components and services and the companies or organisations which they supply.

We may analyse these relations using the following dimensions:

1. Formalisation – the extent to which a transaction between two organisations is 'written down', including the level of detail and the inclusion of penalties.
2. Intensity – this includes
   (a) the amount of resources involved – the proportion of an

organisation's resources committed to a transaction:

(b) the frequency of interaction – the amount of contact between the two organisations.

3. Resource reciprocity – the extent to which resources in a transaction flow to both parties equally or benefit one party alone.

4. Standardisation – the extent of similarity between the two organisations.

Thus a subcontractor which had worked for a contractor over many projects (dimension 2a), where contractual relations are relatively ambiguous (dimension 1), providing skills and resources which the contractor does not possess (dimension 4), would be in an entirely different relation with the main contractor than a new subcontractor (dimension 2b), whose resources became entirely committed to the project (dimension 2a), on what the subcontractor perceived to be a very 'tight' price (dimension 3). Both the relative power of contractor and subcontractor and the commitment of the subcontractor involved would be influenced by the differences in these dimensions. Management of these relations requires good human relations but also a sensitivity to the nature of the relations between the parties. Project management is often a complex process of influence and bargaining in which representatives of the contractor and the subcontractor discuss and bargain over relatively ambiguous problems. For example, the failure of subcontractor A to meet a target date might be partially, or wholly, the result of failures by the main contractor or other subcontractors, or indeed the client. Maintaining co-operative relations on a construction site or other project requires careful attention and cannot be assured through penalty clauses, legal action and the like. The manager must become an effective bargainer.

Whilst we have examined these ideas using the construction industry as an example they may be used to examine any complex project. Thus developments in the telecommunications industry or the oil industry involving a number of organisations, contractors, subcontractors and suppliers, would be similarly amenable to this form of analysis.

Corporatism

Thus far we have examined the role of the organisation in the wider environment, focusing upon how the organisation attempts to govern its own relations, outputs, and so on. In a modern state governments take all manner of direct and indirect actions (with respect to the economy in particular) which influence organisations.

'Corporatism' refers to the way in which government takes an increasingly directive role in relation to industry, directly through mechanisms such as central planning and government, management and union negotiations and discussions, and indirectly through institutions such as, in Britain, the Manpower Services Commission.

The elevation of trade unions and employers' organisations to a new form of status, from interest groups to 'governing institutions', the institutionalisation of mechanisms through which their representatives become involved in the elaboration of policy, are both aspects of corporatism. Whether or not a given state can be described as 'corporatist' is a moot point; however, modern states do exhibit distinct corporatist tendencies.

Whilst there is a great diversity world-wide, there are some trends worthy of note: governments take a role in macro-economic policy, thus affecting competitiveness and productivity, and providing support for strategically important industries. Governments often support investment and represent a major consumer and employer. The extent and form of government ownership vary across the world. Recently governments have established 'joint ventures', with foreign multi-managements, with foreign multinationals. All of this creates new problems and opportunities for managements in both the public and private sectors. Government represents an important aspect of the environment or organisations. The 'corporatist' tendency includes attempts by government to incorporate managers and trade unions into the institutional framework as a means of depoliticising these problems, encouraging co-operation, commitment and national stability and success. These four are seen as the defining characteristics of a corporatist policy.

Corporate affairs, social values and business policy

A view is currently emerging that businesses must take into account the social environment and consequently must look at its moral and ethical standards. Looking at maximum profits and social contributions can often cause conflict in businesses as it adds complexity to strategy formulation and can seem to impinge on creativity. The morality of choice is now part of strategic decision-making.

What is social responsibility?

There are many opinions on the issue of social responsibility and this section will try to highlight the major arguments and opinions. Social responsibility is the concern of business for the welfare of society at large, its obligations beyond the corporation in wider society. These obligations are to some extent governed by legislation. Laws exist to control safety, pollution, rights of employment, and other matters. But responsibility extends beyond this. A business has obligations to shareholders, consumers and the community. The manager today has to consider his acts in relation to society at large. He needs to think beyond the organisation itself and build societal values into his actions. The question is, in pursuing business self-interest, will it or can it lead to benefit the community as a whole?

Let us examine some of the issues surrounding this. One argument would say that business exists through right of privilege. It owns property, and though corporate laws exist, society can change its expectations of what is acceptable and endanger the existence of business. If the consumer for some reason chooses to withdraw support (stop buying a particular product as in a boycott) this will affect profitability and the health of a business. Therefore, a kind of social contract exists between business and society. If the public does not approve of an organisation's product, it will withdraw its support. So the organisation needs to be aware of its public image in order to continue trading.

A more significant example of this can be seen in the activity of pressure groups who work to control and monitor the behaviour of organisations: airline companies which fly jet aircraft, the utilities which operate nuclear power plants, and those firms which manufacture or supply drugs found to be dangerous have all been the target of pressure-group activities. Such activities as these above have an impact upon an organisation's public image and it can rapidly lose public support. Therefore organisations, in their own interests, need to guard against bad publicity. If organisations do not respond to society's demands, then society in turn will withdraw its support. This will affect profitability. However, the control society imposes on organisations must be weighed against other costs. Too much control could damage business and industry, thus producing a negative effect on society, such as unemployment. This has implications as it will then affect the quality of life. Therefore, a balance must be met. Business must be conscious of society's tolerances but society must weigh its demands against other risks, too. How can this be achieved?

Another angle on social responsibility can be addressed. Social responsibility creates an improved environment. As the quality of life improves, conditions become more and more conducive to successful business practice. If wages are high, then purchasing power is increased. As incomes grow, so does the demand for goods and services.

Improvement of public image

If business is seen to be taking a responsible attitude towards the society in which it exists, then its image will be raised. Many organisations are seen to be investing money in improving the environment and increasing educational opportunities through sponsorship schemes, for example. But consider the following example. The anti-smoking campaign has raised public awareness of the health risks involved in smoking. This has led to restricted publicity: a ban on television advertising, and restricted magazine exposure. However, there is continued debate about cigarettes being linked to sports activities via sponsorship, which subtly offers widespread exposure through TV coverage. The interesting point here is the delicate balance between how society restricts and how business responds. The balance is finely drawn between how the public controls and what it will tolerate.

So it is easy to see the relationship between what the public will accept, how it can control business and how far the public can go before destroying the financial fabric which ultimately supports society.

Arguments against social responsibility generally centre around profit maximisation. 'Profitability must be the criterion of all responsible business decisions'. This view is from Peter Drucker (1981) and is argued more strongly by Milton Friedman. Friedman (1962) argues that social responsibility is not the province of corporations. He believes that responsibility should be accorded to stockholders and that it is management's job to make as much money as possible for them. Social responsibility would reduce the return to stockholders. Money spent on social considerations would erode profits which in turn would raise prices, lower wages and have a negative impact on society. Others argue that managers are not trained to deal with social wrongs so that this problem falls outside their responsibility. However, it seems clear that social issues are directly the responsibility of corporations especially in such matters as environmental problems.

Ethical issues

Social responsibility for the business translates into ethical considerations for the individual. It is individuals within organisations who make decisions about the nature and extent of social responsibility and how acceptable the organisation will find these. Ethics relate to the set of standards by which we judge things to be right or wrong. For example, if an organisation does not respond to public pressure to limit its amount of pollutant discharged on the environment, then it is judged on ethical grounds. However, when an organisation is sensitive to public demands and responds accordingly, then the action is seen to contribute directly to human good. Therefore, the organisation's behaviour has a twofold benefit. It cares for the environment and in doing so receives public acclaim and builds a good image for itself.

Business people are expected to act in an ethical manner. If they do not, they run the risk of damaging consumer goodwill and incurring the disapproval of their peers. Gitman and McDaniel (1983) suggest that business ethics comes from five sources: religion, which stresses the dignity of man under God; philosophical systems, which claim reason produces ethical norms; cultural experience, which provides values that society expects to be upheld; legal systems, which should prevent violation of socially accepted ethical standards; and professional codes, which are derived from corporate codes. Codes of ethics are important to the business man as he takes responsibility for the organisation. Individuals are required to make statements and comments which could be embarrassing to the company. Now, the issue becomes how the individual can balance his views and beliefs with a sense of freedom whilst maintaining the interests of his company. Often this is compounded by management's sensitivity and overprotectiveness about the corporation. If the company is to remain productive and creative it must maintain a climate in which the individual enjoys a level of freedom. Overregulation will produce suppression and could result in damaging consequences. Corporate strategists need then to be concerned with a wide range of problems from world issues, community issues and the freedom of the individual within the organisation.

Personal business ethics

Imagine a company which is about to make a number of its workforce redundant. Who is to be made redundant? This is a difficult decision to make but nevertheless a decision must be made. The decision will hinge on the ethical principles of the organisation, and on the values and beliefs of the individuals making the decisions. Gitman and McDaniel (1983) construct a set of principles which might be taken into account when making such decisions: fair treatment of others (justice); the individual's right to be accurately informed of the situation (truth); standing up for what you believe in, even if this has unfavourable consequences (courage); independent thinking and expression (freedom); impartial justice when making decisions about others (fairness); and including others, such as trade unions and employees, in the power process (sharing). Most executives today believe that social responsibility is an ethical issue. Responsibility for the individual and the corporation become social obligations at work and in society at large.

Case study: Nuclear power

Nuclear power technology raises many complex issues. Whatever our personal views on the technology, there is no doubt that it serves as an excellent illustration of the wider impact of organisations on society and on other issues such as the control of technology and the role of governments. The case study selected is a famous accident (the Three Mile Island accident in the USA). This also serves as an illustration of the cause of failure or crisis in organisations. This theme has already been examined in the discussion on 'turnaround' management.

Failure and crisis in organisations

We often say that we learn more from our failures than our successes. Our understanding of organisational effectiveness can be enriched by examining the causes of failures. Whether a failure is associated with the use of technology, or the collapse of a business, a close examination of the events leading up to the failure will identify opportunities which might have been used to forestall the failure. The lack of prior intervention is clearly 'ineffective' behaviour.

Failures may appear to be caused by changes of environmental conditions that organisations cannot control, events may cause severe difficulties for any organisation, and nothing can change that. However, in so far as failures are caused by problems within organisations, these causes are both deep-rooted and important. Environmental change raises questions of how to respond. Competitive pressures may require innovation in product design or production processes. John Child (1984) makes very clear the view that managers are not simply subject to environments but can also respond to them to ensure continued effectiveness.

The study of failures is becoming increasingly part of organisation studies. Much credit for this development must go to Hall (1980) and to an Open University course team (see Bignell, Peters and Pym 1977). Both Child and Bignell *et al.* identify some of the indicators or conditions of failure.

Child (1984, pp.276–8) identifies a number of 'warning signs of a structural problem'. These include overloads of work, poor integration between departments, a reducing capacity for innovation and weakening control. Bignell *et al.*, in their introduction, also develop a number of 'conditions of failure'. Typically the background to a failure will be characterised by the following factors:

1. A situation or a project in which members of several organisations are involved.
2. A complex, ill-defined and prolonged task which gives rise to information difficulties.
3. Ambiguities associated with the way to handle the situation or project (relevant regulations being out of date or not enforced).
4. Members of the organisations concerned operate with stereotyped attitudes with respect to the behaviour of other people and treat complaints from the general public or members of other organisations in a fairly cursory manner, believing them to come from non-experts who do not fully understand the issues involved.
5. Where signs of possible hazards emerge, some will be recognised and planned for but others will be neglected because:
   (a) they are not recognised by those working within a particular occupational or organisational stereotype;
   (b) of pressure of work;
   (c) recognising them and taking action would require the investment of time, money and energy;
   (d) the individuals concerned feel that quite probably it will not happen anyway.

Thus in general 'failures' are characterised by problems of communication, problems of perception and attitudes, problems of uncertainty, inadequacy of procedures for handling the situation and therefore of training. Whilst there is some overlap with Child's list there are important additional factors identified here. We should note, however, that Child was concerned to identify signs of problems stemming from the structure of an organisation whereas Bignell *et al.'s* list deals with conditions for failures generally. We should also note that all failures will not be caused by all of the problems identified above. In looking at the case study we shall see whether or not this 'failure' framework applies. When considering this particular case readers should consider the evidence critically and realistically. Remember the old saying:'There, but for the Grace of God, go I'. In this part of book we are concerned to learn from problems which organisations have experienced rather than to criticise or condemn.

The accident at Three Mile Island

Please remember that no prescription exists to guarantee that accidents or failures do not occur and also that our purpose in presenting the case is not to assign blame or responsibility. The case study is largely based upon the *Report of President Carter's Commission of the Accident at Three Mile Island* (1979). In providing an overall picture of the accident stress will be laid on issues which are of immediate relevance to this book.

Prologue

Three Mile Island is the home of two nuclear power plants, TMI-1 and TMI-2. Together they have a generating capacity of 1,700MW. Each plant is powered by its own nuclear reactor – the reactor performing the function of heating water which, in turn, produces steam, which drives a turbine that turns a generator to produce electricity.

A nuclear reactor generates heat as a result of nuclear fission, the splitting of an atomic nucleus, most often that of the heavy-atom uranium. Uranium fuels all nuclear reactors used commercially to generate electricity in the United States. At TMI-2 the reactor core holds some 100 tons of uranium in the form of uranium oxide, moulded into cylindrical pellets, the pellets stacked one on top of another inside fuel rods (each rod is about 12 feet long). The TMI-2 reactor contained 36,816 fuel rods – 208 in each of its 177 fuel assemblies. A fuel assembly contains not only fuel rods but space for cooling water to flow between the rods and tubes that may contain control rods or instruments.

Control rods contain materials which are strong absorbers of neutrons and which shut off chain reactions. When the control rods are all inserted in the core, fission is blocked. A chain reaction is initiated by withdrawing the control rods. By varying the number of control rods and the length to which they are withdrawn, operators can control how much power a plant produces. The control rods are held by magnetic clamps. In an emergency the magnetic field is broken and the control rods drop into the core to halve fission (a 'scram').

A nuclear plant has three basic safety features, each designed to prevent the release of radiation. The fuel rods themselves trap and hold radioactive materials produced in the uranium fuel pellets. The reactor core is held inside a 40-foot-high steel tank with walls $8^1/_2$ inches thick, surrounded by two heavy concrete and steel shields with a total thickness of up to $9^1/_2$ feet. The reactor coolant system is closed. All this is set inside a containment building, a reinforced concrete structure with walls 4 feet thick.

To supply the steam to drive the turbine, both TMI plants utilise a pressurised water reactor system. It is important that the water heated in the core remains below 'saturation' − the temperature and pressure combination at which water boils and turns to steam. Problems can occur if a significant proportion of the core's coolant water boils away and the core becomes uncovered. In a loss-of-coolant accident (LOCA) the Emergency Core Cooling System (ECCS) automatically uses existing plant equipment to ensure that cooling water covers the core. High-pressure injection (HPI) pumps can pour up to 1,000 gallons per minute into the core to replace cooling water.

Wednesday 28 March 1979

A series of feedwater system pumps supplying water to the TMI-2 steam generator tripped on the morning of 28 March 1979. The nuclear plant was operating at 97 per cent capacity. The first pump trip occurred at 4.00.36 a.m. The plant automatically shut down the steam turbine and electric generator two seconds later.

The process of steam generation removes some of the intense heat that the reactor water carries. When the feedwater flow stopped the temperature of the reactor coolant increased. The water expanded, the water level in the pressuriser tank rose, pressure in the tank built up and a relief valve (PORV) opened. Steam and water began flowing out of the reactor coolant system through a drain pipe and into a tank. Pressure continued to rise and eight seconds after the first pump tripped, TMI-2's reactor scrammed.

Heat generated by fission fell rapidly to zero but the decaying radioactive materials continued to heat the reactor's coolant water. When the feedwater pumps shut down, three emergency feedwater pumps automatically started. Fourteen seconds into the accident an operator in TMI-2's control room noted that the emergency pumps were running but failed to notice the two control panel lights which indicated that a valve was closed on each of the emergency feedwater lines and thus no water could reach the steam generators (one light was covered by a yellow maintenance tag).

Thirteen seconds into the accident with a pressure of 2205 psi (pounds per square inch) the PORV should have closed. It did not. A light on the control panel indicated that an electrical signal had been sent to close the valve, leading the operators to assume that it was closed. But the PORV was stuck open and would remain open for 2 hours 22 minutes draining the cooling water – a LOCA. In the first 100 minutes of the accident some 32,000 gallons (one-third of the capacity of the reactor coolant system) escaped out of the let-down system.

The burden of dealing with the early stages of the TMI accident fell on four men – the shift supervisor in charge of both TMI-1 and TMI-2, the shift foreman for TMI-2 and two control-room operators. The two operators were in the control room when the first alarm sounded, followed by 100 alarms within minutes. The operators reacted quickly according to their training. One operator reported that 'I would have liked to have thrown away the alarm panel. It wasn't giving us any useful information'.

The shift supervisor alerted the TMI-1 control room of the TMI-2 scram and called his shift foreman back to the control room. The shift foreman had been overseeing maintenance on the plant's number seven polisher – one of the machines that remove dissolved minerals from the feedwater system. This repair work may well have triggered the initial pump trip.

With the PORV stuck open and heat being removed by the steam generators, the pressure and temperature of the reactor coolant system dropped. The pressurised water level also dropped and 13 seconds into the accident the operators turned on a pump to add water to the system. The volume of water was shrinking as it cooled and more water was needed to fill the system. Forty-eight seconds into the accident, with pressure falling, the water level in the pressuriser began to rise because the amount of water pumped into the system was greater than that being lost through the PORV.

One minute and 45 seconds into the accident, with their emergency water lines blocked, the steam generators boiled dry, the reactor coolant heated up again, expanded and pushed the pressuriser level up further.

Two minutes into the accident, with the pressuriser level rising, pressure in the reactor coolant system dropped and, automatically, two HPI pumps began pouring around 1,000 gallons per minute into the system. The water level in the pressuriser continued to rise.

Approximately 2 minutes 30 seconds after the HPI pumps began working an operator closed one down and reduced the flow of the second to less than 100 gallons per minute. The falling pressure,

coupled with a constant reactor coolant temperature after HPI came
on, should have alerted the operators that TMI-2 had suffered a
LOCA, and therefore that they should maintain PI. 'The rapidly
increasing pressuriser level at the onset of the accident led me to
believe that the high pressure injection was excessive, and that we
were soon going to have a solid system' (extract from evidence to
the Commission). A 'solid' system is one in which the reactor and
cooling system, including the pressuriser, are filled with water. The
operators had been trained to keep the system from 'going solid',
a condition that would make controlling the pressure within the
reactor coolant system more difficult, and which might result in
damage to the system.

Five and a half minutes into the accident steam bubbles began
forming in the reactor coolant system, displacing coolant water from
the reactor. The displaced water moved into the pressuriser, sending
the pressuriser water level still higher. The operators continued to
believe that there was plenty of water in the system and, moreover,
began draining off the reactor's coolant water through piping called
the let-down system.

Eight minutes into the incident the control room staff discovered
that no emergency feedwater was reaching the steam generators.
An operator scanning the control panel checked to see whether a
pair of emergency feedwater valves were open (called the twelve-
valves', they were always supposed to be open except during a
specific test of the pumps). These two valves were closed. The
operator opened them. These 'twelve-valves' were known to have
been closed two days earlier as part of a routine test. This loss of
emergency feedwater had no significant effect on the outcome of
the accident but this incident added to the complexity of the
situation the operators were striving to control.

During the first two hours of the accident the operators appear
to have ignored vital information. For example the high temperature
in the drain pipe that led from the PORV to a drain tank was
rationalised. An emergency procedure states that a pipe temperature
of 200°F indicates an open PORV. The operators testified that the
pipe temperature normally registered high because either the PORV
or some other valve was leaking slightly. One operator stated: 'I
have seen, in reviewing logs since the accident, approximately 198
degrees. But I can remember instances ... just over 200 degrees.
The operators discussed the significance of the temperature readings.
Recorded data show that they reached 285°F.

At 4.11 a.m. an alarm signalled a high water level in the containment building sump, a clear indication of a leak. The water had

come from the open PORV to a drain tank, finally overflowing into the sump. At 4.20 a.m. instruments showed a higher than normal neutron count inside the core, indicating that steam bubbles were present in the core, and forcing the cooling water away from the fuel rods. During this time, the temperature and pressure inside the containment building rose rapidly from the heat and steam escaping via the PORV. The operators turned on the cooling equipment inside the containment building but failed to recognise these additional signs of LOCA.

At about this time one operator received a call from an auxiliary building. He was told that an instrument there indicated more than six feet of water in the containment building sump.

The superintendent of technical support at TMI-2 arrived at 4.45 a.m. He arrived to find an unexpected situation: 'I felt we were experiencing a very unusual situation, because I had never seen the pressuriser level go high ... and at the same time, pressure being low. They have always performed consistently'. The operators shared this view. They later described the accident as a combination of events they had never experienced, either in operating the plant or in their training simulations.

Shortly after 5.00 a.m. TMI-2's four coolant pumps began vibrating severely. This resulted from pumping steam as well as water and was another unrecognised indication that the reactors' water was boiling into steam. Fearing that the vibration might damage the pumps or the coolant piping, and following training, two of the pumps were shut down at 5.14 a.m. At 5.24 a.m. the two remaining pumps were shut down, thus stopping the forced flow of cooling water through the core.

Following a discussion between senior executives of Metropolitan Edison (the company operating TMI), Babcock & Wilcox (the company which had designed and built TMI-1 and TMI-2) and the TMI station manager, a back-up valve between the PORV and the pressuriser was shut at 6.22 a.m. The loss of coolant was stopped but damage continued. There is evidence to indicate that the water in the reactor was below the top of the core at 6.15 a.m. but high-pressure injection was not initiated until 7.15 a.m.

In the two hours after the trip, periodic alarms warned of low-level radiation in the containment building. After 6.00 a.m. the radiation readings increased markedly. By 6.48 a.m. high radiation levels were being monitored in several areas of TMI-2 and there is evidence indicating that up to two-thirds of the 12-foot-high core stood uncovered. At this time it is estimated that core temperature would have been between 3,500°F and 4,000°F. At 6.54 a.m. a reactor coolant pump was turned on but closed again at 7.13 a.m. because of vibration. Shortly before 7.00 a.m. a site emergency was declared, as required by the emergency plan whenever some event threatens 'an uncontrolled release of radioactivity to the immediate environment'.

Summary of some aspects from the Commission's findings

The Commission came to the conclusion that people in the industry had begun to believe that nuclear power plants were safe in operation. Such plants had been operated for many years and substantial attention paid to safety. The Commission (*Report* 1979) concluded that: 'this attitude must be changed to one that says nuclear power is ... potentially dangerous, and, therefore, one must continually question whether safeguards already in place are sufficient to prevent major accidents'. The Commission argued for a comprehensive system of safeguards in which equipment and human beings were to be treated of equal importance.

It is noted that there seemed to be a preoccupation with regulations, whilst accepting that the Nuclear Regulatory Commission (NRC) was responsible for the development of regulations. However, it took the view that regulations do not assure safety. In fact, they noted that, once regulations become voluminous and complex, they can become a negative factor in safety.

Moreover, they suggested that scientists and engineers in the industry concerned with nuclear power plant safety had become too concerned with major accidents. The question considered was: 'What is the worst kind of equipment failure that can occur'. Many major accident conditions were considered. Such major accidents require fast reactions which many concluded must be handled automatically. Lesser accidents may develop slowly and control may be dependent on the appropriate action of human beings.

Concentrating on the licensing function the Commission noted that the NRC required applicants to consider failures from only single causes. The Commission concluded that the industry had taken the view that equipment could be made 'people-proof'. Thus, not enough attention was paid to the training of operating personnel and procedures.

They also suggested that the NRC was too concerned with licensing and not with the ongoing process of assuring safety. They noted that there existed a divided system of decision-making on important issues, ranging from plant design to safety. For example, control-room design appeared to have been a compromise of the utility, its parent company, the architect-engineer and the supplier.

Most importantly, several earlier warnings that operators needed clear instructions for dealing with events like those during the accident had been disregarded. In September 1977 there had been a similar incident at another plant, also equipped with a B&W reactor. A PORV stuck open, pressuriser level increased and pressure fell. The operators improperly interfered with the HPI. The plant had been operating at only 9 per cent power. A B&W internal memorandum written more than a year before the TMI accident stated that if the September 1977 accident had occurred in a plant operating at full power 'it is quite possible, perhaps probable, that core uncovery and possible fuel damage would have occurred'. No information on appropriate operator procedures was circulated prior to the TMI accident. Nine times before the TMI accident PORVs had stuck open at B&W plants. B&W did not inform its customers of these failures, not did it highlight them in its own training programme.

Finally, the Commission noted that trainees could fail parts of the modular training tests, including sections on emergency procedures and equipment, and still pass and thus qualify as an operator. There were no formal syllabuses or training manuals and little interaction between those conducting the training and those concerned with plant design.

Clearly the case provides an example of how organisations can have a wider impact. But the case also illustrates something of the complexity being faced. Rarely are these issues presented in a simple form. This is certainly the case here. It is worth noting that each of the factors identified in the earlier discussion of 'failure' situations applied in this case. The reader may care to look at the case again to confirm this view.

Here also is a case in which a network of organisations was involved. We have the operator, the main contractor responsible for construction, and the Nuclear Regulatory Commission. The role of the NRC is particularly interesting here. Its staff faced many complex problems in their work. Here we are not concerned to do more than point to the pressures within which people work in these situations.

Concluding comment

In this book a wide range of ideas and concepts about management have been introduced. It is clear that the practice of management is complex. It is just as clear that managers are beset by complex problems. To be successful the manager needs skill and knowledge, intuition and experience, and luck. Whether or not good managers are born, there seems little doubt that management skills and knowledge can be enhanced. More fundamentally management development is a feasible objective. In this book the intention has been to consider some of the problems along the way.

Finally, just as the management task is both complex and fragmented, so it is also evolving. Thus we cannot draw a close on management but rather look forward to more challenge and more change. That is what management is all about!

Bibliography

Adams, J. L. (1987). *Conceptual Blockbusting*, Penguin.

Adams, J. S. (1963). 'Wage Inequalities, Productivity and Quality', *Industrial Relations*, vol. 3, pp. 261–75.

Adams, J. S. (1965). 'Injustice in Social Exchange' in Berkowitz, L. (ed.), *Advances in Experimental Psychology*, vol. 2, Academic Press.

Adams, J., Hayes, J., and Hopson, B. (1976). *Transitions – Understanding and Managing Personal Change*, Martin Robertson.

Alderfer, C. (1969). 'An Empirical Test of New Theory of Human Needs', *Organizational Behaviour and Human Performance*, vol. 14.

Altman, E. I. (1983). *Corporate Financial Distress*, Wiley.

Ansoff, I. (1965). *Corporate Strategy*, Penguin.

Argenti, J. (1976). *Corporate Collapse*, McGraw-Hill.

Argyris, C. (1964). *Integrating the Individual and the Organisation*, Wiley.

Argyris, C. (1982). *Reasoning, Lerning and Action*, Jossey-Bass.

Argyris, C. (1985). *Strategy, Change and Defensive Routines*, Pitman.

Argyris, C., and Schon, D. (1974). *Theory in Practice: Increasing Professional Effectiveness*, Jossey-Bass.

Argyris, C., and Schon, D. (1978). *Organizational Learning – A Theory of Action Perspective*, Addison-Wesley.

Bendix, R. (1956). *Work and Authority in Industry*, Wiley.

Beesley, M., and Evans, P. (1978). *Business Social Responsibility*, Martin Robertson.

Bignell, A., Peters, G., and Pym, C. (1977). *Catastrophic Failures*, Open University Press.

Bruce, R. (1976). *The Entrepreneurs – Strategies, Motivations, Successes and Failures*, Libertarian Books.

Burns, T., and Stalker, G. (1961). *The Management of Innovation*, Tavistock.

Campbell, J. P., Dunnette, M. D., Lawler, E. E., and Weick, K. (1970). *Managerial Behavioural, Performance and Effectivenss*, McGraw-Hill.

Chandler, A. (1962). *Strategy and Structure*, MIT Press.

Channon, E. (1973). *The Strategy and Structure of British Enterprise*, Macmillan.

Child, J. (1984). *Organization: A Guide to Problems and Practice*, Harper and Row, 2nd edition.

Clarke, P. (1972). *Small Businesses – How they Survive and Succeed*, David and Charles.

Cohn, T., and Lindberg, R. A. (1974). *Survival and Growth – Management Strategies for the Small Firm*, AMACOM,

Coleman, D. C. (1969). *Courtaulds: An Economic and Social History*, vols. 1 & 2, Clarendon Press.

Cooper, G. (1981). *Psychology and Management*, Macmillan.

Dalton, G. W., Thompson, P. H., and Price, R. (1977). 'The Four Stages of Professional Careers – A New Look at Performance by Professionals', *Organizational Dynamics*, vol. 6, no. 1, pp. 19–42.

De Vries, M. K. (1980). *Organizational Paradoxes – A Clinical Approaches to Management*, Tavistock.

Drucker, P. F. (1981). 'What is Business Ethics', *The McKinsey Quarterly*, Autumn.

Dubin, R., and Spray, S. L. (1964). 'Executive Behaviour and Interaction'. *Industrial Relations*, vol. 3, pp. 99–108.

Friedman, M. (1962). *Capitalism and Freedom*, University of Chicago Press.

Galbraith, J. W. (1977). *Organization Design*, Addison-Wesley

Gitman, L. J., and McDaniel, C. (1983). *Business World*, Wiley.

Haire, M., Ghiselli, E. E., and Gordon, M. E. (1967). 'A Psychological Study of Pay', *Journal of Applied Psychology*, vol. 5.

Hall, R. (1980). *Organization*, Wiley.

Handy, C. (1984). *Understanding Organizations*, Penguin, 2nd edition.

Hedley, B. (1976). 'A Fundamental Approach to Strategy Development', *Long Range Planning*, December.

Hedley, B. (1977). 'Strategy and Business Portfolio', *Long Range Planning*, February.

Hellreigel, D., Slocum, J. W., and Woodman, R. W. (1986). *Organizational Behaviour*, West Publishing Co., 4th edition.

Herzberg, F. (1966). *Work and the Nature of Man*. Wiley.

Herzberg, F., Mausner, B., and Snyderman, B. B. (1959). *The Motivation to Work*, Wiley.

Hofstede, G. (1968). *The Game of Budget Control*, Tavistock.

Horne, J. H., and Lupton, T. (1965). 'The Work Activities of Middle Managers', *Journal of Management Studies*, vol. 12, pp. 14–33.

Jacques, E. (1976). *Bureaucracy*, Weidenfeld and Nicolson.

Kanawaty, J. (1976). *Managing and Developing New Forms of Work Organisation*, 1st edition, ILO.

Kanter, R. (1983). *The Change Masters*, George Allen & Unwin.

Kharbanda, D. P., and Stallworthy, E. A. (1986). *Management Disasters and How to Prevent Them*, Gower.

Kingston, W. (1977). *Innovation, the Creative Impulse in Human Development*, John Calder.

Kirkpatrick, D. (1985). *How to Manage Change Effectively*, Jossey-Bass.

Kissinger, H. (1979). *The White House Years*, Weidenfeld and Nicolson.

Kunloff, A. H. (1966). *Reality in Management*, McGraw-Hill.

Lawler, E. (1978). *Motivation and Work Organizations*, Brooks Cole Free Press.

Lawrence, P. R., and Dyer, D. (1983). *Renewing American Industry*, Free Press.

Lawrence, P. R., and Lorsch, J. (1967). *Organization and Environment*, Richard D. Irwin.

Lissem, R. (1986). 'Becoming a Metapreneur', *Journal of General Management*, vol. 11, no. 4, Summer.

Lloyd, T. (1986). *Dinosaur and Co: Studies in Corporate Failure*, Penguin.

London, M., and Strumpf, G. (1982). *Managing Careers*, Addison-Wesley.

Lorsch, J. W. (1970). 'Introduction to the Structural Design of Organizations' in Dalton, G., Lawrence, P. R., and Lorsch J. W. (eds) *Organizational Structure and Design*, Irwin-Dorsey.

MacMillan, K. (1986). 'Strategy: An Introduction', *Journal of General Management*, vol. 11, no. 3, Spring.

Maslow, A. (1954). *Motivation and Personality*, Harper.

March, J. G., and Simon, H. A. (1958). *Organization*, Wiley.

McClelland, D. C. (1951). 'Measuring Motivation in Fantasy: The Achievement Motive' in Guetzkow, H. (ed), *Groups, Leadership and Men*, Carnegie Press.

McClelland, D. C. (1961). *The Achieving Society*, Van Nostrand Reinhold.

Merton, R. K. (1940). 'Bureaucratic Structure and Personality', *Social Forces*, vol. 18.

Miller, D., and De Vries, K. (1985). *The Neurotic Organization*, Jossey-Bass.

Mintzberg, H. (1973). *The Nature of Managerial Work*, Harper and Row.

Mintzberg, H. (1983). *Structure in Fives*, Prentice Hall.

Ouchi, W. (1981). *Theory Z*, Addison-Wesley.

Peters, T., and Austin, N. K. (1985). *A Passion for Excellence*, Random House.

Peters, T., and Waterman, R. (1982). *In Search of Excellence*, Harper and Row.

Pollard, S. J. (1965). *The Genesis of Modern Management*, Penguin.

Porter, L. W. (1964). *Organizational Patterns of Managerial Job Attitudes*, American Foundation for Management Research.

Porter, L. W., Lawler, E. E., and Hackman, R. (1975). *Behaviour in Organizations*, McGraw-Hill.

Quinn, J. B. (1979). 'Stratigic Goals: Processes and Politics', *Sloan Management Review*, vol. 19.

Report of President Carter's Commission on the Accident at Three Mile Island (1979), Pergamon.

Revans, R. W. (1971). *Developing Effective Managers: A New Approach to Business Education*, Longman.

Rickards, T. (1985). *Stimulating Innovation*, Frances Pinter.

Robinson, S. J. Q., Hichens, R. E., and Wade, D. P. (1978). 'The Directional Policy Matrix – Tool for Strategic Planning', *Long Range Planning*, June.

Roethlisberger, F. J., and Dickson, W. J. (1939). *Management and the Worker*, Harvard University Press.

Scott, B. R. (1971). *Strategies for Corporate Development*, Harvard Business School.

Slatter, S. (1986). *Corporate Recovery: A Guide to Turnaround Management*, Penguin.

Smith, A. H. (1969). *The Money Game*, Michael Joseph.

Stewart, R. (1977). *Managers and their Jobs*, Macmillan.

Stewart, R. (1982). *Choices for the Manager: A Guide to Managerial Work and Behaviour*, McGraw-Hill.

Storey, D. J. (1982). *Entrepreneurship and the New Firm*, Croom Helm.

Strauss, G. (1976). 'Organizational Development' in Dubin, R. (ed), *Handbook of Work, Organisations and Society*, Rand McNally.

Super, D. E. (1980). *The Psychology of Careers*, Harper and Row.

Tavsky, C., and Parke, E. L. (1976). 'Job Enrichment, Need Theory and Reinforcement Theory' in Dubin, R., *Handbook of Work, Organisation and Society*, Rand McNally.

Taylor, B. (1983). 'Turnaround – Recovery and Growth', *Journal of General Management*, vol. 8, no. 2.

Taylor, B. (1984). 'Strategic Planning – Which Style do you Need?', *Long Range Planning*, June.

Taylor, F. W. (1911). *Introduction to the Principles of Scientific Management*, Jonathan Cape.

Thomas, R. E. (1973). *The Government of Business*, Phillip Allan.

Toffler, A. (1970). *Future Shock*, Bodley Head.

Toffler, A. (1970). *The Third Wave*, Collins.

Vroom, V. (1964). *Work and Motivation*, Wiley.

Walker, J. (1976). *Staff Appraisal and Development*, Allen & Unwin.

Woodward, J. (1965). *Industrial Organization, Theory and Practice*, Oxford University Press.

Index